Aim of this book is to introduce and teach android OS fundamentals in a simple, concise and an easy to implement way as possible.

Android Firmware Customization

Arvind Choudhary

Ashish Verma

ZORBA BOOKS

Published in India by Zorba Books, 2015

Website: www.zorbabooks.com
Email: info@zorbabooks.com

Copyright © Arvind Choudhary

ISBN 978-93-85020-29-2

All rights reserved. No part of this book may be reproduced or transmitted in any form or by any means, electronic or mechanical, including photocopying, recording, or by an information storage and retrieval system—except by a reviewer who may quote brief passages in a review to be printed in a magazine, newspaper, or on the Web—without permission in writing from the copyright owner.

Although the author and publisher have made every effort to ensure the accuracy and completeness of information contained in this book, we assume no responsibility for errors, inaccuracies, omissions, or any inconsistencies herein. Any slights on people, places, or organizations are unintentional.

Zorba Books Pvt. Ltd. (opc)
Gurgaon, INDIA

Cover design by Qualcom Design

Printed in India

Acknowledgement

My family especially my father, Babu Lal Choudhary, who has encouraged me to immerse myself in android research and development field. All my years of Android research has been one of my most enjoyable part of life.

    I should like to express thanks to all my friends especially Ashish Kumar, Abhinaya Pratap Singh, Shiv Mahesh Maurya, Rajendra Verma, who continuously provoke me to include new experiences with Andriod system to be included in this book and have always encouraged me to enhance android research relevancy.

    I am thankful to all my friends and family for their persistence in requesting publication of this edition sooner rather than later.

Arvind Choudhary

Contents

Unit 1: Introduction
- What is android — 1
- Mobile os/firmware in market — 1
- Types of android devices — 1
- Android features — 2
- Android versions — 3
- Android version features — 3
- Android architecture — 9

Unit 2: Architecture
- HAL Layer — 13
- Low level android Architecture — 13
- Audio Architecture — 15
- Bluetooth Architecture — 17
- Media Architecture — 19
- Sensor Architecture — 21
- Batching — 22
- Sensor types — 22
- Graphics Architecture — 23
- DRM Architecture — 25
- Storage Architecture — 26
- I/O Architecture — 28

Unit 3: ADB Commands
- What is adb Command — 30
- Run adb Commands in android — 31
- Android adb command Syntax — 32
- adb devices command — 32
- adb push command — 33
- adb pull command — 33

- adb reboot command   34
- adb reboot recovery command   34
- adb reboot-boot loader command   35
- fastboot command   35
- fastboot oem unlock command   36
- fastboot flash recovery command   36
- adb restore command   37
- adb sideload command   37
- Install apk file   38
- Uninstall apk file   38
- adb remount command   39
- adb logcat command   39
- adb kill server and start server command   40
- adb backup   40
- adb restore command   41

Unit 4: Android adb Shell Commands

- What is shell command   43
- Check root status   43
- Su Command   44
- ls Command   44
- cd command   45
- cp command   45
- cat command   46
- move command   46
- rm command   47
- mount file system command   47
- exit command   48

Unit 5: Activity Manager Commands

- What is Activity manager commands   49
- Start activity command   49
- Start service command   57

- Kill package command — 57
- Kill all service command — 58
- Broadcast command — 58
- Force stop command — 59
- Instrument command — 59
- Debug app command — 60
- Clear debug app command — 60
- Monitor command — 60
- Screen compact command — 61
- Change screen size — 61
- Change screen density — 62

Unit 6: Package Manager Commands
- What is Package Manager Commands — 63
- List package command — 63
- List permission group command — 64
- List instrumentation command — 65
- System features command — 65
- List libraries — 66
- List users — 66
- Apk path — 66
- Install Application — 67
- Uninstall Application — 68
- Clear package — 68
- Enable package or component — 69
- Disable package or component — 69
- Grant permission — 69
- Set install location — 70

Unit 7: Screenshot and screen recoding
- Screenshot — 71
- Screenshot with adb command — 71
- screen Recording — 72

- set size of screen recording 73
- set bit rate of screen recording 74
- set time limit of screen recording 74
- set rotation of screen recording 75
- verbose 75

Unit 8: Other Commands
- UI/Application Exerciser Monkey command 76
- Sqlite database command 76
- Other adb command 77
- Other shell command 77

Unit 9: dumpsys Commands
- EMEI No/Phone Information 79
- Device battery 79
- Wifi 80
- CPU 80
- Location 80
- Disk Memory 81
- Network 81
- Provider 82
- User Permission 82
- Process and PID 83
- Account 83
- Activities 84
- Window 84
- Alarm 85
- GFX 85
- Surface Flinger 86
- Storage Manager 86
- Network Management 87
- Notification 87
- Application Widget 88
- Audio 88

- Backup 89
- Clipboard 89
- Content 90
- Input Method 90
- Camera 91
- Storage 91
- Player 92
- Power 92
- Search 93
- Sensor 93
- Status Bar 94
- Gesture 94
- Wallpaper 95

Unit 10: Key Layout

- Key Layout 96
- Key Layout storage Location 96
- Key Declaration 97
- Keyboard Keys 97
- Joystick Keys 107
- Input Key Event 107

Unit 11: Android Testing

- Android testing 109
- Unit testing 109
- JUnit testing 109
- Monkey testing 110
- Device testing structure 110
- Monkey testing feature 110
- Monkey testing with shell command for device 111
- Monkey testing with shell command for application 111
- Run same event again in monkey testing 112
- Monkey testing with event time 112

- Monkey testing touch event percentage   113
- Monkey testing with motion event percentage   113
- Monkey testing with any event percentage   114
- Monkey testing No of event percentage   114
- Monkey testing ignore crashes   114
- Monkey testing ignore timeouts   115
- Monkey testing ignore security exceptions   115

Unit 12: Android Rom and Structure
- Android rom   117
- Types of rom   117
- Custom rom   117
- Advantage of custom rom   117
- Disadvantage of custom rom   117
- Android rom Structure   118
- Stock rom   119
- Structure and extract stock rom   119
- MTK rom   122
- Structure of MTK rom   122
- Structure and extract Rockchip rom   123

Unit 13: Structure and extract boot, bootloader, recovery and system file
- Boot file   125
- Structure boot file   125
- Extract and repack boot file   127
- Recovery File   129
- Recovery File Structure   129
- Extract and repack recovery file   130
- System file   133
- Extract and repack system file   133
- Bootloader file   136
- Structure of boot loader file   136

- Extract and repack bootloader file — 136
- Extract and repack boot file in ubuntu — 137
- Extract and repack recovery file in ubuntu — 140
- Extract and repack system file in ubuntu — 141

Unit 14: Android rooting
- What is android rooting — 143
- Rooting advantages — 143
- Rooting disadvantages — 143
- How to check device root or not — 144
- How to root — 145
- Internally root — 145
- Externally root — 147

Unit 15: Boot animation
- Boot animation — 150
- Structure of boot animation — 151
- Create boot animation — 153
- Change boot animation in rom — 154
- Change boot animation with adb command — 155

Unit 16: Boot logo
- Boot logo — 156
- Boot logo in stock rom — 156
- Create and change first boot logo in stock rom — 157
- Create and change second boot logo in stock rom — 159
- Boot logo in mtk rom — 164
- Create and change first boot logo in mtk rom — 165
- Create and change second boot logo in mtk rom — 168
- Boot logo in rockchip rom — 172
- Create and change boot logo in rockchip rom — 172

Unit 17: Install android rom
- Install Device driver — 174
- Install stock rom by live suit tool — 180
- Install stock rom by phoenix card tool — 182
- Install MTk rom by sp flash tool — 185
- Install rockchip rom by batch tool — 188

Unit 18: Other Custmization
- Build.prop file — 192
- Default.prop file — 198
- Add and remove system apps — 199
- System libraries — 201
- System permission — 201
- Break pattern and password locl — 202

Unit 19: android os programming
- Root checker — 204
- Root checker externally — 204
- Root checker internally — 205
- Boot animation creator — 205
- Boot animation changer — 211
- Create system application — 213
- Remove system application — 213
- Copy system application — 214
- Reboot device — 214
- Reboot to recovery — 214
- Reboot to bootloader — 215
- Power off device — 215
- Factory reset device — 216
- Storage management — 216
- Set as system memory by default — 216
- Set as internal memory by default — 216
- Set as external memory by default — 217

Unit 1: Introduction

- **What is Android?**

Android is Linux based operating system Developed by Google for android devices with java interface. Android developed for touch screen Devices like mobile and tablet. Android is also an open source Alliance. It mean each user can customize android firmware. We can see that each manufacture customize android os and provide different UI to user. This operating system take input through touch it may be resistive or capacitive from user and provide solution according to user input. Android is popular with technology because provide low-cost and customizable operating system for high-tech devices.

It is pure open source. For example, an application can call any of the phone's core functionality such as making calls, sending text messages, or using the camera.

Android is built on the open Linux Kernel. It utilizes virtual machine (Dalvik virtual machine) that was designed for optimize memory and hardware resources in a mobile environment.

Android does not different between the phone's core applications or system applications and third-party applications. They can have equal access to a phone's capabilities.

Android provides wide range of useful libraries and tools that can be used to build applications. For example, Android enables developers to Developed access the location of the device, and allows devices to communicate with one another social applications.

- **Mobile OS/Firmware in Market**

There are lot mobile operating devices available in market. Each os Developed by Different Languages are as follows:
Samsung old –bada, J2Me.
Nokia old-Simbian.
Blackberry-blackberry.
I Phone, I paid (Apple)-IOS.
Nokia new-Windows.
HTC, LG, Samsung, Micromax , Lemon, Carbon, Lava-android.

- **Types of Android Devices**

There are lot of android devices available in market like Smartphone, tablet, television (android TV), car (Android Auto),

Digital Camera, glasses. These devices are very cheap and easy to use and change lifestyle of human being.

- **Android Features**

Messaging

Android provide two types of messaging SMS and MMS.SMS provide text messaging android MMS provide image audio and Video Messaging it also provide C2DM messaging. C2DM provide cloud to device messaging. It provides push notification from server to registered device.

Web browser

Android web browser provides open source web kit.

Voice Features

Android provide voice based feature for text, voice and calling.

Multi-touch

Android also provide multi-touch feature.

Multitasking

We can do multiple tasks at a time with android, for example we can listen music and chat together at same time.

Calling

Android include two types of calling features audio and video.

Multiple language support

Android support multiple language.

Bluetooth and Wifi support

Android support Bluetooth and wifi which provide communication between deferent devices. Bluetooth send text, audio and video files between two devices and wifi provide internet data connectivity.

Wifi Hotspot

Wi-Fi Hotspot connects internet data to other device.

Media

Android provide media support also like png, jpg, Gif, bmp (image) mp3, mp4, amr.wav (audio and video) formats.

Screen Capture and Screen Recording

Android provide screen capture facility in all version and screen recording in kit-Kat and upper version.

Data Storage

Android also provide data storage facility. There are three data storage facility first one is os storage which contain app and system files second one is internal data storage it provide internal memory for data storage and third one is external storage.

Sqlite
Sqlite use data storage in android application. It is a light weight database.

- **Android versions**

Name	Version	API level
Alfa	1.0	1
Beta	1.1	2
Cupcake	1.5	3
Donut	1.6	4
Éclair	2.0-2.1	5,6,7
Froyo	2.2-2.2.3	8
Gingerbread	2.3-2.3.7	9,10
Honeycomb	3.0-3.2.6	11,12,13
Ice Cream Sandwich	4.0-4.0.4	14,15
Jelly Bean	4.1-4.3.1	16,17,18
Kit Kat	4.4-4.4.4	19,20
Lollipop	5.0-5.1	21,22

- **Android version features**

Android 1.0
- Android market
- Web browser
- Camera
- Home screen
- Gmail
- Google contacts
- Google map
- Google search
- Google talk
- SMS and MMS
- Media player
- wifi
- Bluetooth
- YouTube
- Alarm clock
- Calculator

- Dialer
- Gallery
- Setting

Android 1.1
- User business search on map
- User can attach on messages

Android 1.5: cupcake
- Support third party keyboard
- Video recording
- Paring in Bluetooth
- Copy and paste in web Brower
- Use picture in contact
- Attach date time in call log
- Auto rotation
- New stock boot animation
- Ability to upload videos to YouTube

Android 1.6: donut
- Voice and text entry to search
- Speech synthesis
- Easier searching
- Advance gallery and camera
- Text to speech engine
- Support for WVGA screen resolution
- Expand gesture framework

Android 2.0-2.1: Eclair
- Expand account sync
- Bluetooth 2.1 support
- Ability to tap a contact and select call sms and email
- Improve camera like flash support , digital zoom, scene mode
- Improve typing speed of virtual keyboard
- Browser Ui with thumbnail
- Optimize hardware speed
- Support more screen size and resolution
- Improve Google map
- Live wallpaper

Android 2.2-2.2.3:Froyo
- Enhance speed and memory
- Add java script with browser

- Add c2dm
- Improved launcher app
- Add wifi tethering and wifi hotspot
- User can disable data access
- Add multiple keyboard facility
- Improved Bluetooth
- Add password facility
- Enhance app memory
- Adobe flash support
- Add zoom gesture with gallery

Android 2.3-2.3.7: Gingerbread
- Updated user interface
- Add WXGA screen resolution
- Faster and improve virtual keyboard
- Add copy/paste function
- Support NFC
- New download manager
- Add front and back end camera
- Improved power management
- Improve native development code
- Improve audio graphics and input
- Increase performance
- Add more sensors
- Add new api
- Add Google talk
- Add lib support for peripheral device
- Improve network performance
- Improve Gmail app
- Improve camera
- Improve battery efficiency
- Add Google wallet

Android 3.0-3.2.6: Honeycomb
- Add new holographic user interface
- Add system bar
- Add action bar
- Add multitasking
- Redesign keyboard, fast typing
- More function into coy/paste
- Add multiple tab in browser
- New function in camera like focus flash zoom

- Hardware acceleration
- Support multiple core process
- Add ability to encrypt data
- Add secondary memory
- Add recent app list
- Resizable home screen
- Support external keyboard
- High performance wifi lock
- Improve hardware support
- Ability to access app to sdcard
- Add new function to display
- Improve android market
- Improve Google book
- Improve adobe flash

Android 4.0-4.0.4: Ice Cream Sandwich
- Add holo interface
- Separation of widget in a new tab
- Improve visual voicemail
- Pinch to zoom function in calendar
- Add screenshot capture
- Add lock screen
- Improve copy paste
- Improve voice integration
- Add face lock feature
- Enable and disable data
- Ability to close recent app
- Improve camera app
- Built in photo editor
- New gallery layout
- Add NFC
- Hardware acceleration of the UI
- Numerous bug fix and optimization
- Improve to graphics, database, spell checking
- New api for developer
- Improve calendar app
- Improve camera app add QVGA
- Better camera performance
- Smooth screen rotation
- Improve phone no reorganization

Android 4.1-4.3.1: Jelly Bean
- Blue tooth low energy support
- Add ability to transfer audio/video to Bluetooth
- OpenGL support
- Dial paid auto complete
- Volume for incoming call
- Rework camera UI
- Smoother UI
- Improve accessibility
- Expandable notification
- Ability to turn off notification
- Shortcut and rearrange widget
- Bluetooth data transfer for beam
- Improve camera app
- Multichannel audio
- USB audio
- Ability to add other launcher
- Lock home screen rotation support
- Lock screen improve
- Notification power Control
- Screensaver
- Multiple user account
- New clock app
- Group messaging
- Fixed Bluetooth audio streaming bug
- Quick setting
- New download notification
- New alert for low battery
- New gallery app animation
- USb debug white list
- Bugfix and improvement
- Improve security
- System level support for geofencing and wifi scanning api
- Add support more language
- Change DRM api
- Clock display in status bar

Android 4.4-4.4.4: Kit Kat
- Improve clock app
- Ability to app to trigger translucency
- Ability to use app in immersive mode

- Menu button always visible
- Improve performance
- Wireless printing
- Improve web view
- Expand notification listener service
- New framework UI
- Audio tunneling and audio monitoring
- Screen recording feature
- Native infrared blaster api
- Bluetooth message access profile support
- Improve auto focus
- Better app compatibility
- Camera app can load google+ photo
- Bugfix
- Refreshed dialer app interface
- Release smart watches
- UI updates for Google map navigation and alarm
- Offline playback
- GPS support

Android 5.0-5.1.1: Lollypop
- Support 64 bit CPU
- OpenGL ES 3.1
- Add material design
- Refreshed lock screen
- Refreshed notification
- Quick search
- Lock screen with shortcut
- Audio and video input with USB
- Third party can read and modify sdcard data
- Recent app remembered after reboot
- Web view receiver update through Google play
- Add 15 new languages
- flash light style app include
- add smart lock
- few bug fix
- quick control on wifi and Bluetooth form setting
- support multiple sim card
- device protection
- high definition voice call

- improve notification priority
- fix memory leak issue

- **Android Architecture**

Android operating system architecture is a stack of software components like applications, an operating system, run-time environment, middleware, services and libraries. In this architecture each layer communicates with other layer for execution of process.

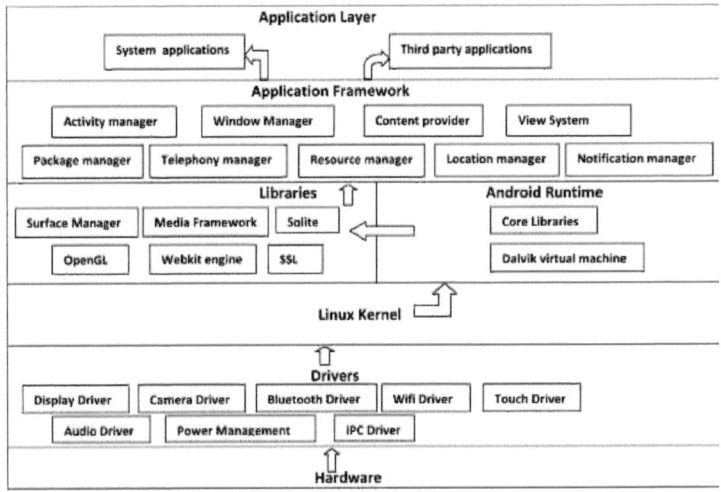

Application Layer

This is most upper layer in android architecture. This layer contains all Application of devices. There are two types of applications first types are system applications like phone contact Messaging and second types are third party applications which are install externally or form play store. System application cannot be Uninstall but Third party application can uninstall by user from device.

Application framework

This is second layer of android structure. This layer contain set of service which are required for android activity and reuse by other applications like that if we want to perform calling so we will have to need telephony manager service to perform this task. So there are lot of other service just like activity manager perform activity task and lifecycle, window manger perform system UI, content provide manage share set of data of device like contact and massage, system view manage application widget, package manager manage all install application packages, resource manager other resource like string, color and layout, location manager manage map related functions, notification manager alert all system notification like battery, massage, location.

Libraries
This layer divides in to two parts one is android libraries and second is android runtime. Libraries contain java based and C/C++ libraries. Java libraries contain lot of libraries.

Java libraries
- android.app – this library has fully model of android application.
- Android.view – this library provide user interface to user.
- android.widget – this library provide user interface component for application like button, edit text etc.
- android.webkit – this library contain all classes regarding web server.
- android.os – this library contain all classes for os just like message passing between activity messaging.
- android.media – this library contain media classes.
- android.openGL – this library contain 3D graphic classes.
- Android.provider – this library provides classes for share set of database or predefined database.
- android.content – this library contain all classes to use transfer data form one activity to other activity.
- android.database – this library contain all classes to use store data of any application.
- android.graphics – this library contain all classes for graphic 2D and 3D.
- android.hardware – this library contain all classes to interact with hardware like sensor.
- android.net – this library contain app classes for network programming.
- android.util – this library contain all classes for string data conversion and collection framework.

C/C++ libraries
This library contains slandered libraries of C/C++.this libraries communicate between android driver and android libraries because

all drivers developed with C/C++ libraries. This library also used for NDK (native development kit).

Android Runtime
It is a type of JVM used in android devices to run apps and optimized for low processing power and low memory environments. Android runtime contain core libraries which communicate with kernel. Dvm provide environment for multitask execution. Each task execute directly by kernel in android.

Linux kernel
The basic layer is the Linux Kernel. Fourth layer of android architecture is Linux kernel which provides communication between hardware and software. The whole Android OS is built on top of the Linux Kernel. Kernel means the core of Operating System. Linux kernel that interacts with the hardware and it contains all the essential hardware drivers.

Drivers are programs that communicate with the hardware. For example all devices has a Bluetooth hardware in it. Therefore the kernel must include a Bluetooth driver to communicate with the Bluetooth hardware.

Android drivers
This is the fifth layer of android architecture. This layer provides all drivers which are necessary for android device. Android drivers communicate between hardware and Linux kernel. Drivers recognize hardware and perform talk with software or we can say that it perform exactly what we want with hardware for example suppose we want to extend out device memory for this task we will need flash memory driver which recognize external memory then process to software.

Android hardware
This is the last layer of android architecture which contains device hardware. We can easily understand by this diagram

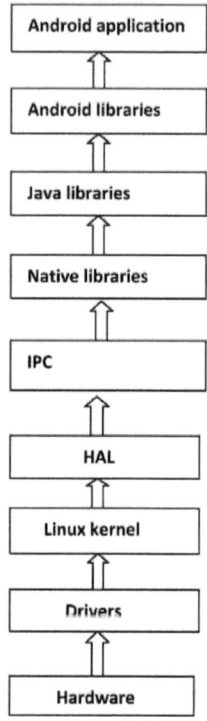

From above Diagram we can easily understand that the execution of any task done from bottom to top. For example supposes we want perform any action on our device then firstly we will intact with device hardware with touch screen or any other hardware. then screen recognize what action have you perform and hardware interact with driver according you requirement for example if you want to play music then will goes to audio driver or if want use wifi it goes to wifi driver. Then driver interact with libraries with help of Linux kernel then process will be forward to Native libraries and native libraries. Because Native libraries used to develop android operating system files then it forward to java android libraries to execute process. Java libraries contain core libraries android libraries predefined classes just like calling messaging etc., then finally application perform task.

Unit 2: Architecture

In this chapter we will discuss different architecture like HAL, Media, Bluetooth, DRM and etc. These things are necessary to know before learn about android firmware.

- **HAL (Hardware Abstraction Layer)**

It is the main layer of android architecture. This layer provides Communication between hardware and software mean that it provide communication between android driver and android service. Android open source provide facility that you can download android software and customize this software according to your requirement. HAL contain audio, graphics, wifi, Bluetooth, camera, media and storage drivers.

Low Level android Architecture

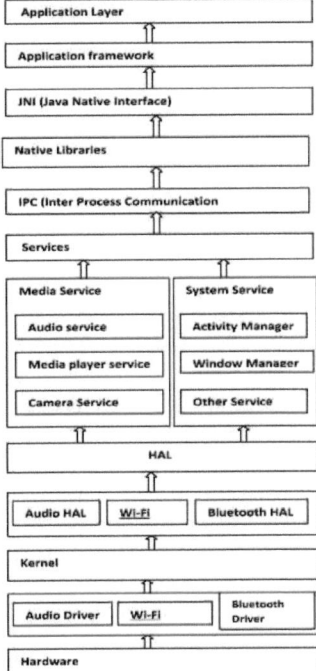

Application Layer
This Layer has all application including system and third party application. Application Layer provide User interface to user that interact directly to user for example contact, messaging, calling etc.

Application Framework
Android framework provides API to provide android libraries to user applications. Application may be system applications or third party applications.

JNI (java native Interface)
JNI provide core code for android libraries or android API.

Native Libraries
Native libraries provide interface to system API. This files are written in c/c++ code.

IPC (Inter Process Communication)
IPC provide Communication between different processes.

Services
Services are bang round process which are provide interface between API. There are two types of services system service and media service. System service includes Window, notification and media service includes Media Player and Media Recording.

HAL (Hardware Abstraction Layer)
HAL provide communication between hardware with software. It is provide Interface with your hardware and drives.

Kernel
Linux processes any task with provide resources with adding hardware and software. It is the link of hardware and software.

Drivers
This layer provides all drivers which are necessary for android device. Android drivers communicate between hardware and Linux kernel. Drivers recognize hardware and perform talk with software or we can say that it perform exactly what we want with hardware for example suppose we want to extend out device memory for this task we will need flash memory driver which recognize external memory then process to software.

- **Audio Architecture**

Audio Architecture has mainly two process media player and media recording.

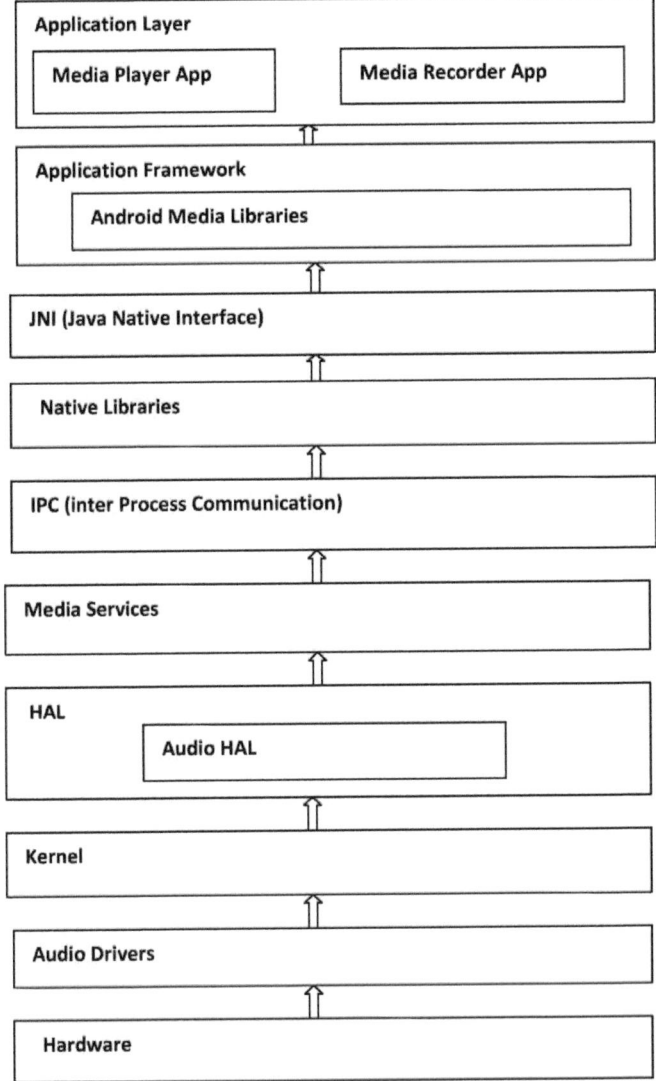

Application Layer
Application layer of audio architecture include media player application and media recording application.

Application framework Layer
Android framework layer include **android.media**library which access JNI.

JNI
JNI access by Application framework layer and it contain java core code. It is located in to **framework/base/core/jni** and **framework/base/media/jni** folder.

Native Libraries
Native libraries contain c/c++ core libraries which communicate with android.media API. It is located in **framework/av/media/libmedia**.

IPC (Inter process Communication)
Ipc provide communication between different processes. It is also located in **framework/av/media/libmedia**.

Media Service
Media service provide interface with HAL. It is located in **framework/av/services/audio flinger**.

HAL
HAL provide interface with audio hardware component with audio HAL. It is located in **device/vendor/product/audio**.

Karan
The Main work of Kernel is that executes process and provide interface with driver with native code.

Driver
Driver layer contain audio drivers.

- **Bluetooth Architecture**

Bluetooth architecture executes all Bluetooth related application and provides API to third party applications.

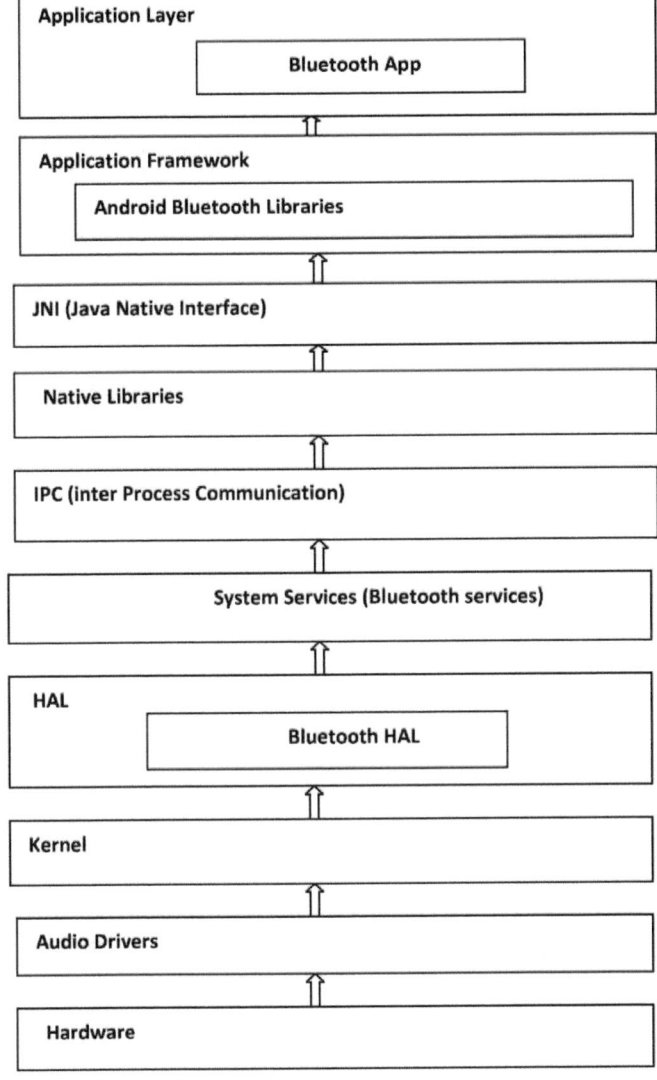

Application Layer
Application layer of audio architecture include Bluetooth applications.

Application framework Layer
Android framework layer include **android.bluetooth** Libraries which access JNI and interact with Bluetooth hardware.

JNI
JNI access by Application framework layer and it contain java core code. It is located in **package/app/Bluetooth/jni.**

Native Libraries
Native libraries contain c/c++ core libraries which communicate with android.bluetooth API.

IPC (Inter process Communication)
Ipc provide communication between different processes.

System Service
Media service provide interface with HAL. It is located in **package/app/Bluetooth.**

HAL
HAL provide interface with audio hardware component with android.bluetooth libraries. It is located in **hardware/libhardware/include/hardware.**

Keranl
The Main work of Kernel is that executes process and provide interface with driver with native code.

Driver
Driver layer contain Bluetooth drivers.

- **Media Architecture**

In media architecture executes all media application and provides API to third party applications.

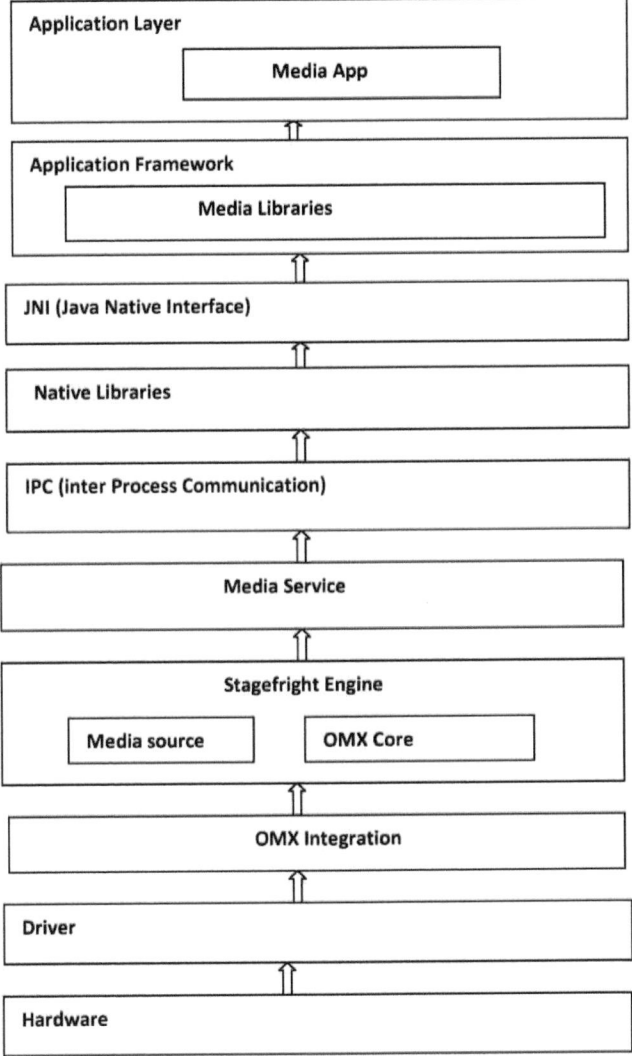

Application Layer
Application layer of audio architecture include media applications.

Application framework Layer
Android framework layer include **android.media** Libraries which access JNI.

JNI (java native Interface)
JNI provide core code for android libraries or android API.

Native Libraries
Native libraries provide interface to system API. This files are written in c/c++ code.

IPC (Inter Process Communication)
IPC provide Communication between different processes. It is also located in **framework/av/libmedia.**

Media Service
It is multimedia framework which provide engine for audio and video Record. For this process use mediaplayerservice.cpp and located in to **framework/av/media/libmediaframewrokservice.**

OMX Integration
OMX Integration provides interface with hardware based component.

• Sensors Architecture

Sensors Architecture executes all applications which are related Sensors.

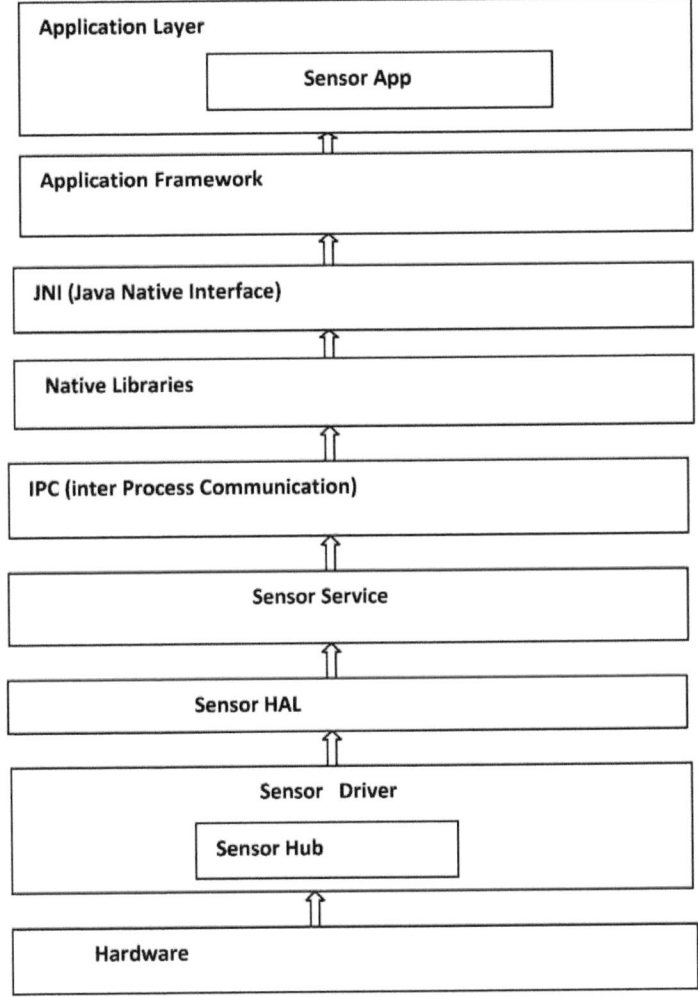

Application layer of audio architecture include Sensor applications.

Application framework Layer
Android framework layer include **android.hardware** Libraries which access JNI and interact with Bluetooth hardware.

JNI (java native Interface)
JNI provide core code for android libraries or android API. Its provide interface with **android.hardware**API. This include in **frameworks/base/core/jn**i folder.

Native Libraries
Native libraries provide interface to system api. This files are written in c/c++ code. This include in **frameworks/native** folder.

IPC (Inter Process Communication)
IPC provide Communication between different processes.

Sensor Service
Sensor service provide interface with HAL.

Sensor HAL
Sensor HAL provides user space.It is provide Interface with your hardware and drives. Its contain sensors.h and sensors.app files. It's located in to **hardware/libhardware/include/hardware.**

Sensor Driver
Sensor driver contain input event and sensor hub driver which understand by kernel.

Sensor Hub
Sensor hub use in low levelcomputation.

- **Batching**

Batching process is used to store sensor event in hardware in FIFO to process to HAL.

- **Sensor Types**

Base Sensor
This type's sensor associate with hardware
1) ACCELEROMETER
2) GYROSCOPE
3) MAGNETOMETER

Composite Sensors
Sensor which not associates with base sensor is called composite sensor.

- **Graphics Architecture**

Graphics Architecture executes all applications which are related with 2D and 3D graphics.

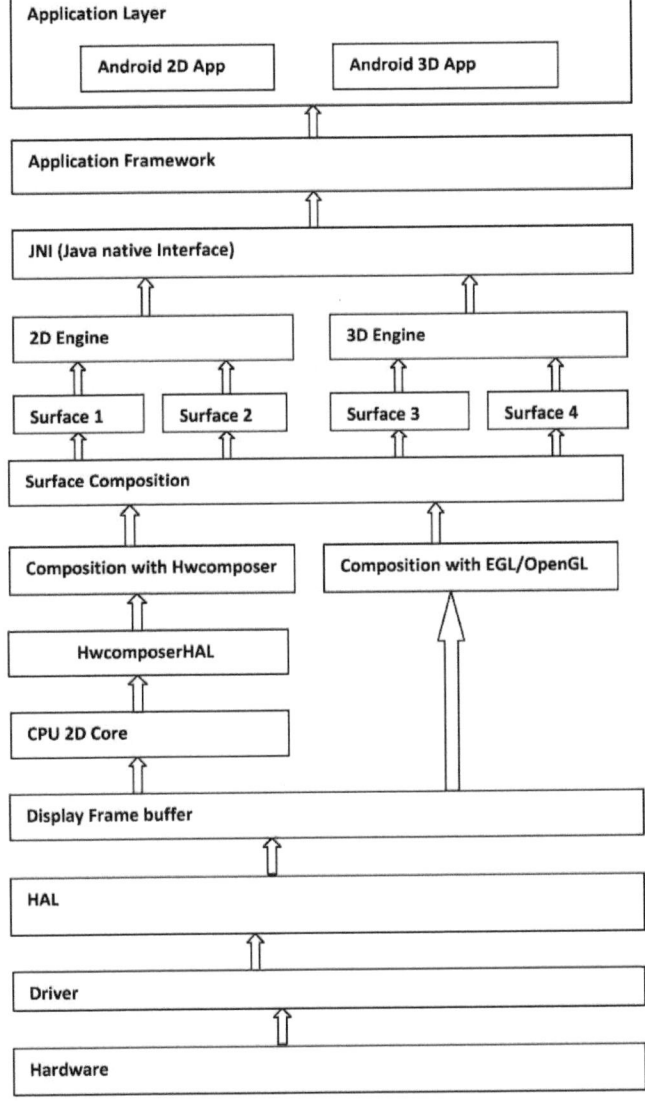

Application Layer
This layer contain media player app, camera applications, OpenGL app.

Application Framework
This Layer includes window Manager Lib and OpenGL lib.

JNI (java native Interface)
This layer contains core code like surface.cpp, GLConsumer.cpp files in **frameworks/native/lib/gui** folder.

2D and 3D Engine
This layer contain java lib for 2d and 3d Graphics.

Composition with HwComposer
HwComposer used to combine specific surface layer supported by specific vendor. And Hwcoposer Disable by removing/ **System/lib/hw/hwComposer.imx6.so**. It's a hardware lib file.

HwComposer HAL
HwComposer HAL Layer provide interface HwComposer with CPU 2D core layer.

Display Frame Buffer
Frame buffer display take input from hardware and provide output to display. For this used to high speed semiconductor.

Modern Graphics System

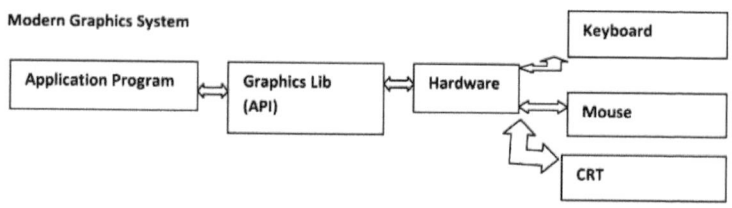

From above figure we can easily understand Application access graphics and android graphics lib contain openGL or Direct3D lib. Its provide communication between application part and hardware part and hardware part provide input to system.

- **DRM Architecture**

DRM is an acronym for Digital Rights Management. Android developers include DRM licenses in applications that protect their best interests. The DRM framework on your Android device makes the use of DRM licenses possible. Android DRM licensing is free service offered to Android application developers who publish apps through the Android Market.

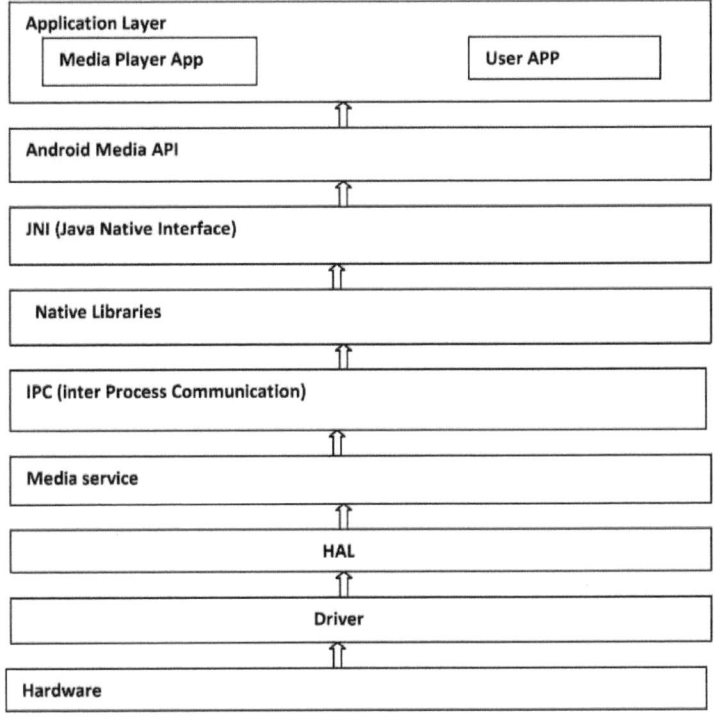

Application Layer
Application layer contain many android app which provide interface with application framework layer.

Application Framework
Application framework layer contain **android.media.mediacrypto** API which access by application layer.

JNI
This API contain core code of c/c++ code. It is located in **frameworks/base/media/jni** folder.

Native API
Native API associate with JNI API and it located into **frameworks/av/media** folder.

IPC
IPC provide directly link between different processes. Its contain Icrypto.cpp and Imedia*.cpp and it's located in to frameworks/av/include/media directory.

Media Service
Media service provide interface with HAL it contain in Crypto.cpp. It is located in **frameworks/av/media.**

- **Storage Architecture**

Storage Architecture provides storage API to third party Applications.

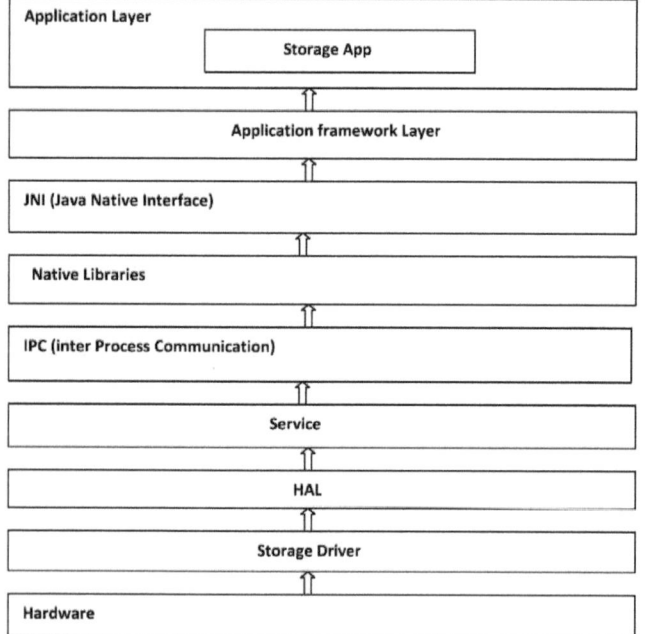

Application Layer
This is most upper layer which can contain many storage applications like file manager etc.

Application framework Layer
This is the second layer of storage Architecture which contains Android storage API like content provider. For this Layer used **android.os.storage** lib.

JNI (Java Native Interface)
This Are java lib which provide interface between native lib android lib.

Native Libraries
Native Libraries is most important layer in this architecture. Native Libraries provide interface between java lib android IPC because both IPC and java lib used this layer.

IPC
IPC provide communication between native lib and different Applications.

Service
This layer contain Mount Services which provide declare memory related all Information about device.

HAL
HAL layer is most important layer in this architecture which provides communication between android driver part and application part.

Driver
Driver layer contain many android driver which provide interface between hardware part and low Level application part.

- **I/O Architecture**

Input/output Architecture provides all APIS for Input/output data access by this party application.

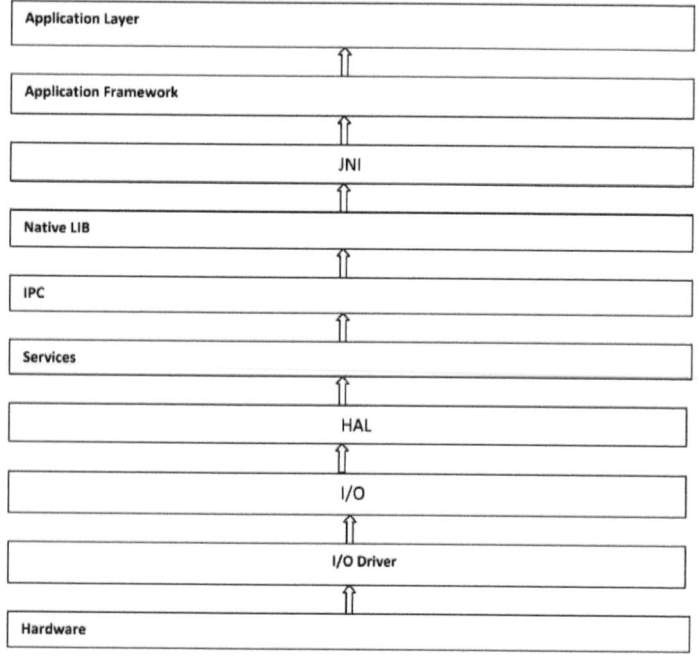

Application Layer
Application Layer is most upper layer in android I/O Architecture. This Layer Contain many Application for input Declaration like that touch screen or game, Key layout mostly all applications.

Application Framework Layer
Application framework layer Support application layer and provide android libraries to application layer.

JNI
Java native libraries are java libraries which support to android libraries like 2D and 3D graphics, openGL.

Native Libraries
Next Level is native libraries which support to java or we can say that access by java native library.

IPC (Inter Process Communication)
IPC provide Communication between different processes which provide link between applications.

Services
This layer contain all services to related devices it may be system services or server services depend on talk which do you want to be execute.

HAL
HAL layer perform linking between to layer or we can say that it's associate hardware and low level software layer.

I/o Layer
This layer provides input to device by software. We may provide input by touch screen or key layout we will learn about key layout later.

Unit: 3 ABD Commands

In this chapter we will discuss about android adb commands like root check devices, remount command, reboot command, boot loader, reboot recovery etc.which are necessary for any developer or any android user.

- **What is ADB Commands**

Adb (android debug bridge) are command which provide communication with android device or emulator or we can control whole device with commands. We can interact with rom through adb commands. Like In pc we can interact with kernel level through cmd commands as at same we can interact at kernel level by adb commands. Some commands may work or not because all device control through by provide root and devices read write permission. We can provide root in our device by two types first by externally and second by internally we will learn deep later about rooting. This command may work on some device and may be not in some device the reason behind this because we can see there is lots of different-different rom available in currently in market like stock rom, Rockchip rom, mtk rom ete. Each rom directory structure is different .There are two types of commands we find in android adb command and shell command.

Adb file in android device located in/system/bin directory.

In below picture we can see adb file in device

Name	Date modified	Type	Size
adb	7/22/2015 4:33 PM	File	111 KB
aee	7/22/2015 4:33 PM	File	14 KB
aee_aed	7/22/2015 4:33 PM	File	82 KB
aee_core_forwarder	7/22/2015 4:33 PM	File	10 KB
aee_dumpstate	7/22/2015 4:33 PM	File	22 KB
akmd8963	7/22/2015 4:33 PM	File	34 KB
akmd8975	7/22/2015 4:33 PM	File	30 KB
akmd09911	7/22/2015 4:33 PM	File	42 KB
am	7/22/2015 4:33 PM	File	1 KB
ami304d	7/22/2015 4:33 PM	File	30 KB
app_process	7/22/2015 4:33 PM	File	10 KB
applypatch	7/22/2015 4:33 PM	File	53 KB
atrace	7/22/2015 4:33 PM	File	10 KB
badblocks	7/22/2015 4:33 PM	File	22 KB
batterywarning	7/22/2015 4:33 PM	File	6 KB
bmgr	7/22/2015 4:33 PM	File	1 KB
bmm050d	7/22/2015 4:33 PM	File	58 KB
boot_logo_updater	7/22/2015 4:33 PM	File	10 KB
bootanimation	7/22/2015 4:33 PM	File	34 KB
btconfig	7/22/2015 4:33 PM	File	14 KB
btlogmask	7/22/2015 4:33 PM	File	6 KB
bu	7/22/2015 4:33 PM	File	1 KB
bugmailer.sh	7/22/2015 4:33 PM	SH File	2 KB
bugreport	7/22/2015 4:33 PM	File	6 KB

Unit 3: ABD Commands | 31

- **Run adb Commands in android**

There are following step to apply to execute adb command.
1) For adb commands firstly you will have to connect your device through usb debugging mode or you will have to on usb debugging to going developer option in setting application in device.

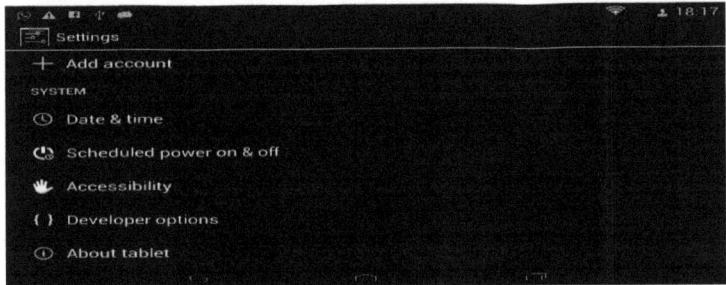

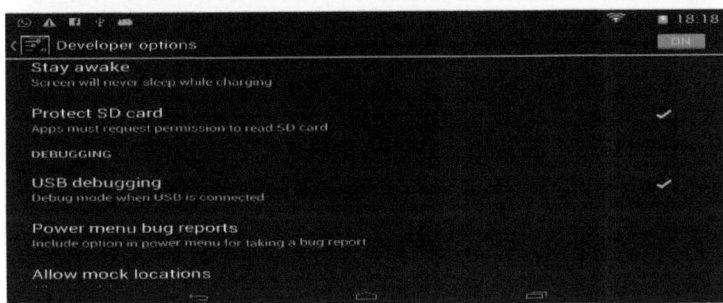

2) Next connect your device with system by usb cable.
3) Go to platform-tools folder in press ctrl+shift and right click there.

4) Press open command window here.

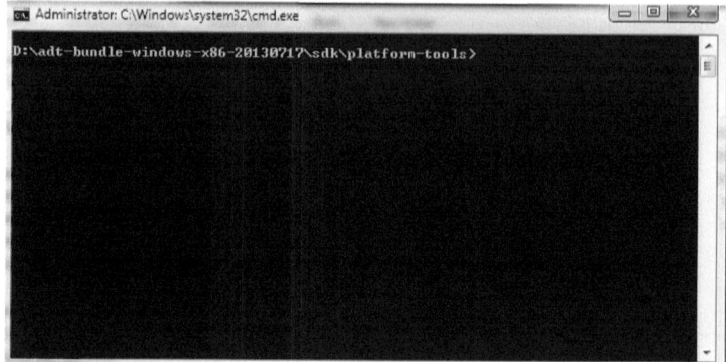

- **Android adb command Syntax**

If single device is connected with system no need to specify it but if more than one device are attached with system you will have to specify target device by d, e, and s.

Ex: adb [-d|-e|-s <serial no><command>

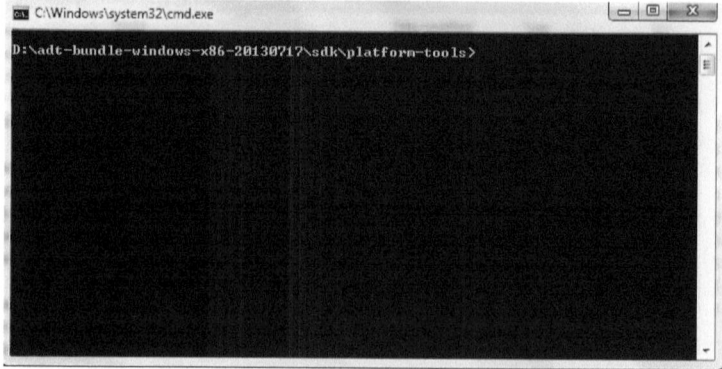

- **adb device command**

To check how many devices are connected with your pcso we run this command.

Unit 3: ABD Commands | 33

Ex: adb devices

```
C:\Windows\system32\cmd.exe

D:\adt-bundle-windows-x86-20130717\sdk\platform-tools>adb devices
List of devices attached
0123456789ABCDEF        device

D:\adt-bundle-windows-x86-20130717\sdk\platform-tools>
```

- **adb push command**

adb push command use to move a file from your pc to android devices.

Ex: adb push <path of source file><path of destination file>

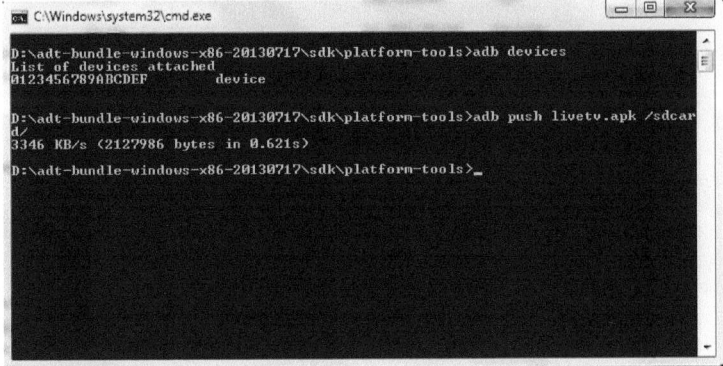

- **adb pull Commands**

adb push command use to move a file from your device to pc.

Ex: adb pull <path of destination file><path of source file>

- **adb Reboot command**

Ex: adb reboot
adb reboot command use to restart your device or we can say boot again.

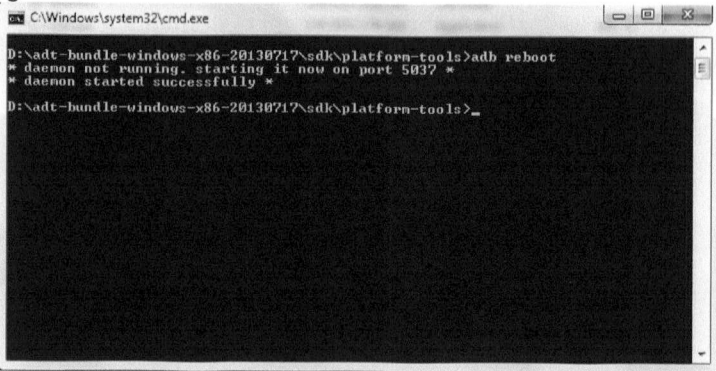

- **adb reboot recovery command**

If you want to go in device recovery mode you will have to use adb recovery command. With help of this command you can change your device setting like reboot or if you want to install any shell script or flashing Rom.

Unit 3: ABD Commands | 35

Ex: adb reboot recovery

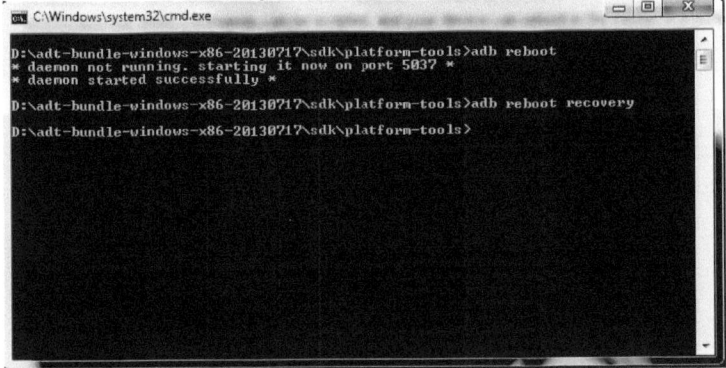

- **adb reboot-bootloader command**

This command use to reboot your device in to bootloader mode (white screen with android wheels). Once you are in bootloader, ADB Won't work anymore.

Ex: adb reboot-bootloader

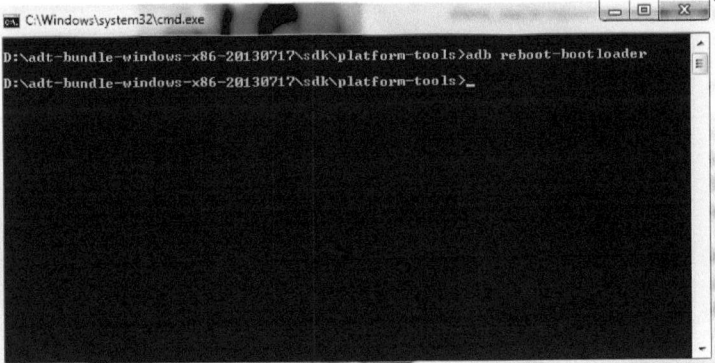

- **Fastboot command**

Fastboot command use to unlock your and modify your device.

Ex: fastboot devices

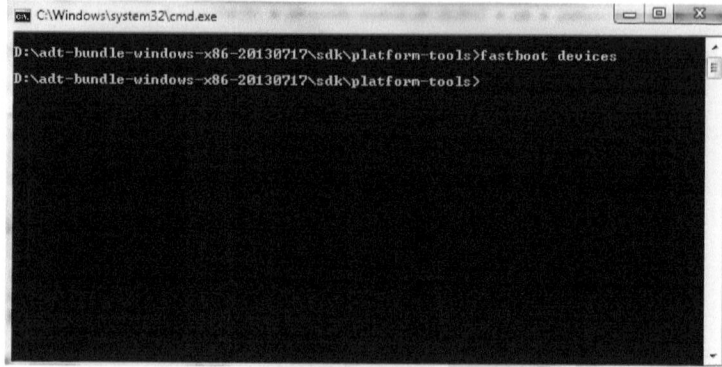

- **fastboot oem unlock command**

fastboot oem unlock command use to unlock you bootloader and make possible to root access. In some device like nexus your device needs to root access or super user permission you will have to need this command to do it.

Ex: fastboot oem unlock

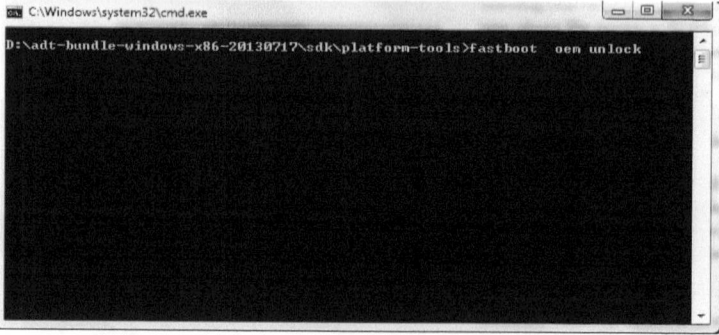

- **fastboot flash recovery command**

fastboot flash recovery command to use flash custom recovery image to your device.

Ex: fastboot flash recovery

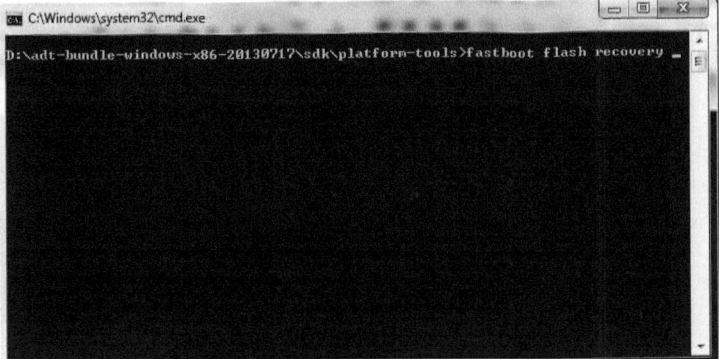

- **adb restore command**

adb restore command use to restore and back your device all data in form of zip file.

Ex: adb restore C:\[restorefile].zip

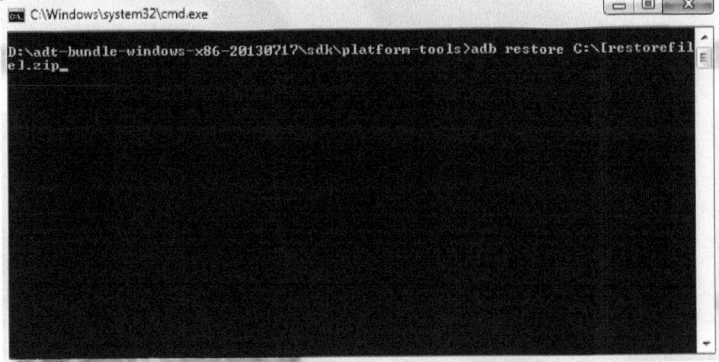

- **adb sideload command**

adb sideload command use to push and flash android custom rom and zip file in your device. With help of this command we can put your rom zip file in to your device and starts flash it.

Ex: adb sideload<path of zip file>

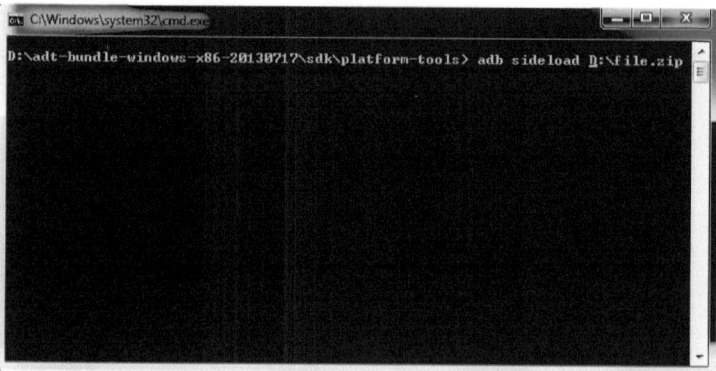

- **Install apk file**

If you want to push an apk in your device and install to it so we use install install apk command.

Ex: adb install <apk path>

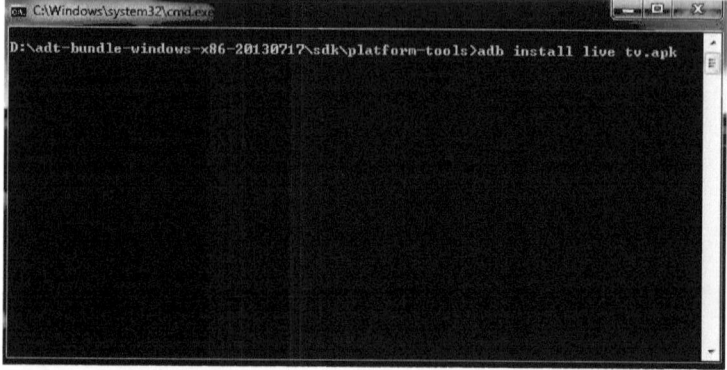

- **Uninstall apk file**

We can unstill also an apk file using unstill apk adb commands

Unit 3: ABD Commands | 39

Ex:adb unstill <package name>

```
C:\Windows\system32\cmd.exe

D:\adt-bundle-windows-x86-20130717\sdk\platform-tools>adb devices
List of devices attached
0123456789ABCDEF        device

D:\adt-bundle-windows-x86-20130717\sdk\platform-tools>adb uninstall com.demo.hel
lo
Success

D:\adt-bundle-windows-x86-20130717\sdk\platform-tools>_
```

- **adb remount command**

Sometime you may be need to read write permission so adb remount command use to remount the system partition in your dive and provide device to read and write permission.

Ex: adb remount

- **adb logcat command**

This command mostly use in android debugging your android device. When you start your device various process running in your device or in other word various log run in your device so this command use to view various log.

Ex: adb logcat

```
D/NativeCrypto( 1093): Doing SSL_write() with 2333 bytes to go ssl=0x51c620b0, a
ppData=0x509bca90
D/NativeCrypto( 1093): Returned from SSL_write() with result 2040, error code 0
ssl=0x51c620b0, appData=0x509bca90
D/NativeCrypto( 1093): Doing SSL_write() with 285 bytes to go ssl=0x51c620b0, ap
pData=0x509bca90
D/NativeCrypto( 1093): Returned from SSL_write() with result 285, error code 0 s
sl=0x51c620b0, appData=0x509bca90
D/NativeCrypto( 1093): ssl=0x51c620b0 sslWrite buf=0x4171b0b8 len=490 write_time
out_millis=0
D/NativeCrypto( 1093): Doing SSL_write() with 490 bytes to go ssl=0x51c620b0, ap
pData=0x509bca90
D/NativeCrypto( 1093): Returned from SSL_write() with result 490, error code 0 s
sl=0x51c620b0, appData=0x509bca90
I/System.out( 1093): <doSendRequest
D/NativeCrypto( 1093): ssl=0x51c620b0 sslRead buf=0x413521c0 len=8192,timeo=3000
0
D/NativeCrypto( 1093): Doing SSL_Read() ssl=0x51c620b0, appData=0x509bca90
D/NativeCrypto( 1093): Returned from SSL_Read() with result -1, error code 2 ssl
=0x51c620b0, appData=0x509bca90
D/NativeCrypto( 1093): sslSelect type=READ fd=62 appData=0x509bca90 timeout_mill
is=30000
D/IPCThreadState( 555): [DN #5] BR_CLEAR_DEATH_NOTIFICATION_DONE cookie 0x59c07
fb0
```

- **adb kill server and start server command**

Sometime your adb may be stuck so this is the common problem so you kill your adb with this command. And again you can start your adb with start server command.

Ex: adb kill-server Ex: adb start-server

```
D:\adt-bundle-windows-x86-20130717\sdk\platform-tools>adb kill-server

D:\adt-bundle-windows-x86-20130717\sdk\platform-tools>adb start-server
* daemon not running. starting it now on port 5037 *
* daemon started successfully *

D:\adt-bundle-windows-x86-20130717\sdk\platform-tools>
```

- **adb backup**

This command use to take all data backup in database file .db

Unit 3: ABD Commands | 41

Ex:adb backup all –f /temp/backup.db

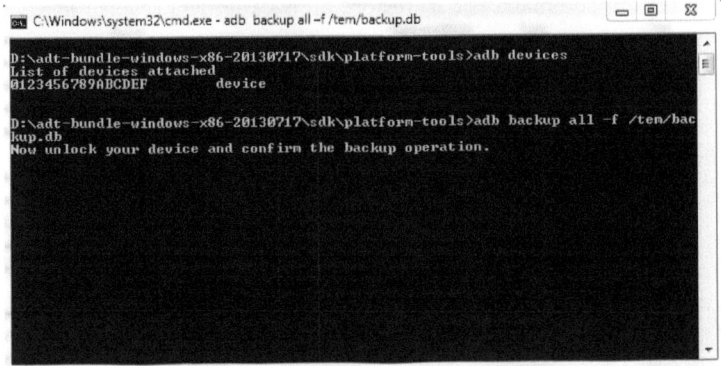

From above picture this command unlocks your device and takes backup in form of database.

- **adb restore command**

adb restore command use to restore all backup data reverse in your device.

Ex: adb restore /tem/backup.db

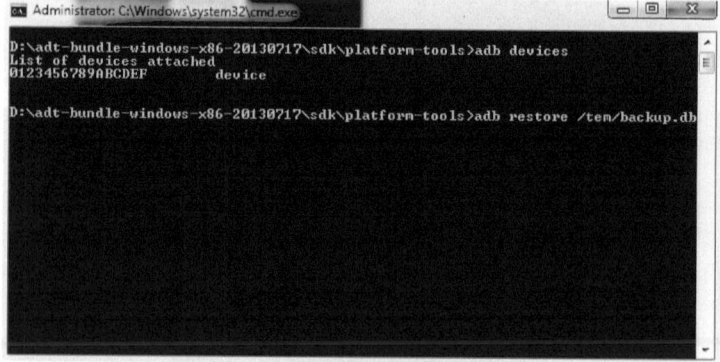

Unit 4 : Android ADB Shell Commands

In this chapter we will discuss about android shell commands like root status, ls command, cp command etc., which are necessary for any developer or any android user.

- **What is shell command?**

Shell is programs that listen to keyboard input from user and display output to user. We run shell command like cmd command in system. If our device is rooted we can read, write and edit system file with shell command. This contain in system/bin/ directory. This command may work on some device and may be not in some device the reason behind this because we can see there is lots of different-different rom available in currently in market like stock rom, Rockchip rom, mtk rom etc. Each rom directory structure is different.

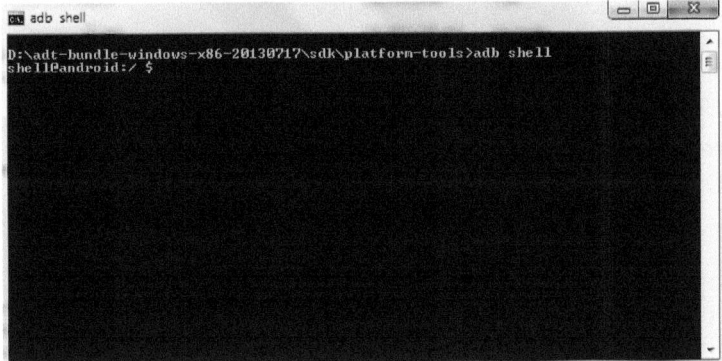

- **Check root status**

This command checks this device is root status. Rooting is break manufacture limitation in device. We will learn about rooting in next chapter. From above figure we can see that shell@android:/$ in output this sign indicate that device is non rooted device if it will be shell@android:/# than it will be rooted device.

Su Command

Ex: adb shell su

Su command indicate that this device provide super user permission to user. If device use a super user we can do anything with device or we can modify device according to our requirement.

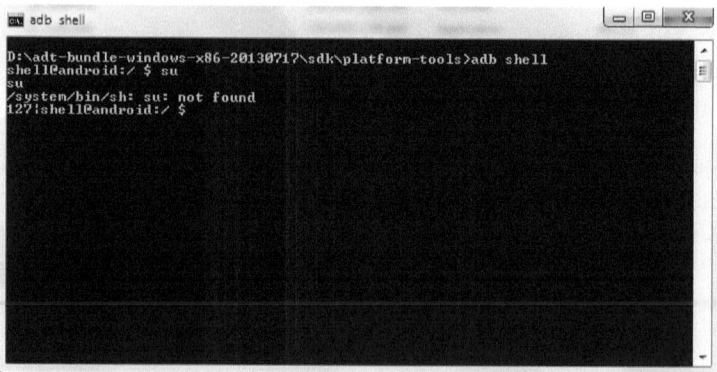

From above picture we can see clearly that su file not found in/system/bin directory this indicate that device has no power permission to super user.

ls shell Command

ls command use to find all folder and files in directory.

Ex:adb shell ls

From this picture we can see that these are all directories and files in root directory.

cd shell command

cd command use to switch from one directory to other directory or from current directory to other directory.

Ex: cd <current directory><other directory>

```
D:\adt-bundle-windows-x86-20130717\sdk\platform-tools>adb shell
shell@android:/ $ cd system
cd system
shell@android:/system $
```

cp shell command

cp command use to copy data from one directory to other or we can say that its copy data from system to device or device to system.

Ex: mv /system/app/example.apk > /sdcard/example.apk

```
D:\adt-bundle-windows-x86-20130717\sdk\platform-tools>adb shell
adb server is out of date.  killing...
* daemon started successfully *
shell@android:/ $ cp system/app/AppStats.apk sdcard
cp system/app/AppStats.apk sdcard
shell@android:/ $
```

In above picture we copy data from system app to sdcard.

cat shell command

cat command also use to copy data from one directory to other or we can say that its copy data from system to device or device to system.

Ex: cat<source path><destination path>

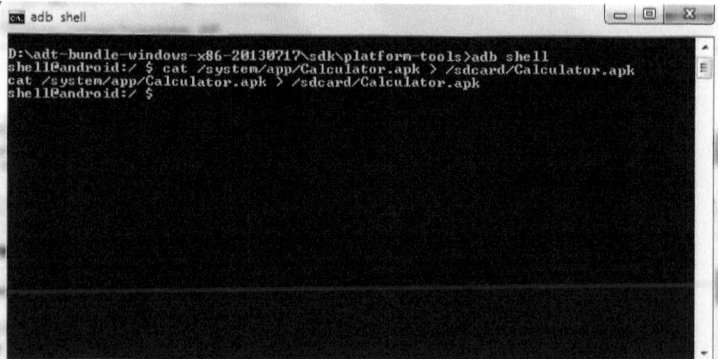

Move Command

It is also format of copy command .it move file from source to destination.

Ex: mv /system/app/SystemUI.apk /sdcard/ SystemUI.apk

rm Command

rm command use to remove any directory or ant file from device.

Ex: rm <path of the file>

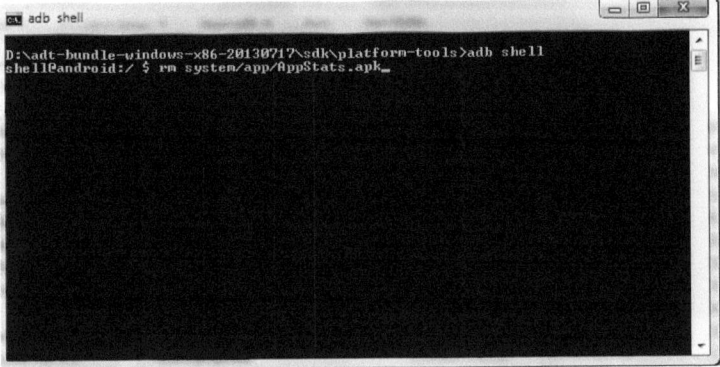

Mount Files system command

Mount file system command use to mount the partition to read/write for file in device we can say that it's provide read/write permission to device.

Ex: mount –o rw,remount -t ysffs2 /dev/block/mtdblock3 <path of directory>

exit command

exit command use for exit from shell command.

Ex: exit

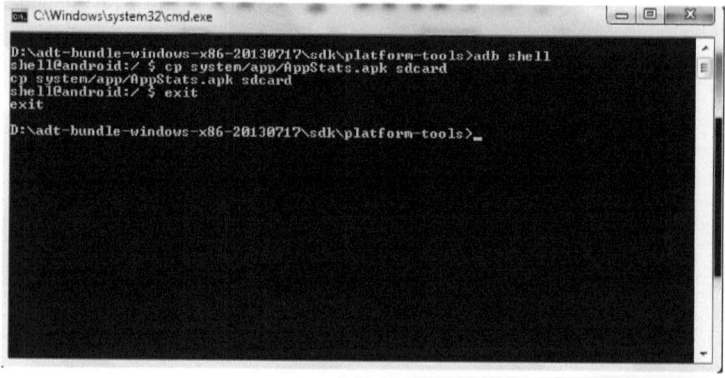

Unit: 5 Activity Manager Commands

In this chapter we will learn about different activity manger command. For this commands we can know all information about any device application activities.

- **What is Activity manager commands**

Activity manager commands are adb shell commands which is use for any application Activity and these commands perform many actions with activity. This command are use to start an activity, stop any activity, broadcast any intent modify ant device screen properties and many more.

And syntax is.

am<command>

Activity manager commands start with am syntax. The may be include intent specification.

<intent> Specification includes these Flags:
-a: <ACTION>
-d :< DATA_URI>
-c :< CATEGORY>
-t :< MIME_TYPE>
-e :< EXTRA_KEY>
--es:<EXTRA_STRING_VALUE>
--esn: <EXTRA_KEY>
--ez:<EXTRA_KEY><EXTRA_BOOLEAN_VALUE>
-n :< COMPONENT>
-f: <FLAGS>

- **Start Activity command**

If we want start any activity from adb commands so use start activity command for it.

ex: am start <package name>/.<activity name>

or

am start<intent>

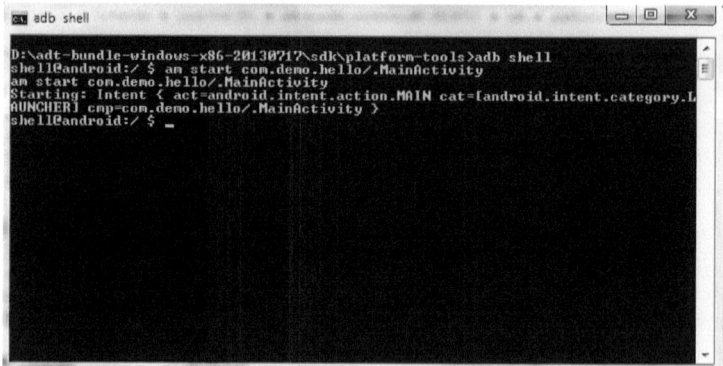

We can open menu using start with help of intent.

This am command will open complete action menu of your device. For this we pass access intent and start will initiate intent. We just need to know what kind of intent we need.

Ex: am start <Intent>

And output of the this command is below.

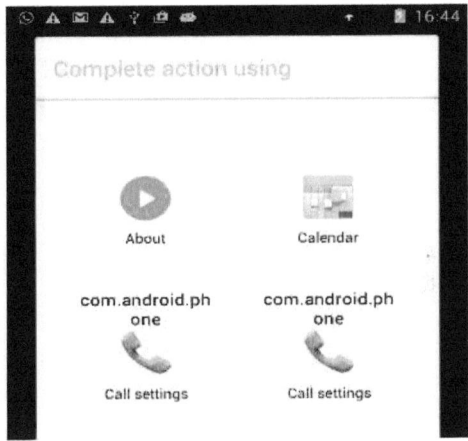

We can also open a web page using am start command.

Ex: am start http://www.google.com

```
D:\adt-bundle-windows-x86-20130717\sdk\platform-tools>adb shell
shell@android:/ $ am start http://www.google.com
am start http://www.google.com
Starting: Intent { act=android.intent.action.VIEW dat=http://www.google.com }
Warning: Activity not started, its current task has been brought to the front
shell@android:/ $
```

And output of this command is in below picture.

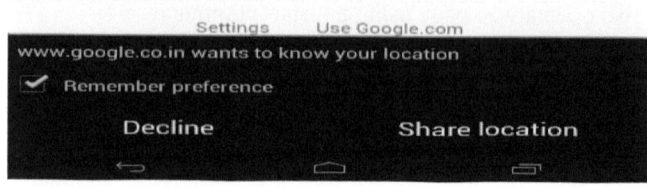

We can open map and find out current location of our device.

Ex: am start geo: 0,0q=Delhi, India

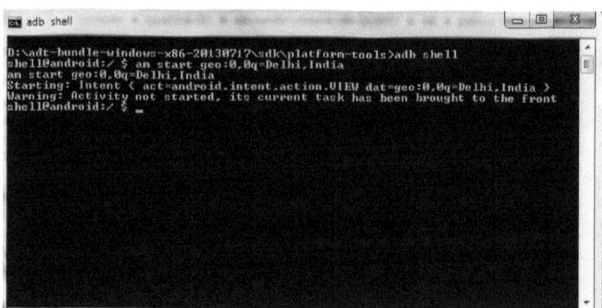

And output of this command is

You can also add, edit or view your device contacts.

Ex: am start content: //contacts/people

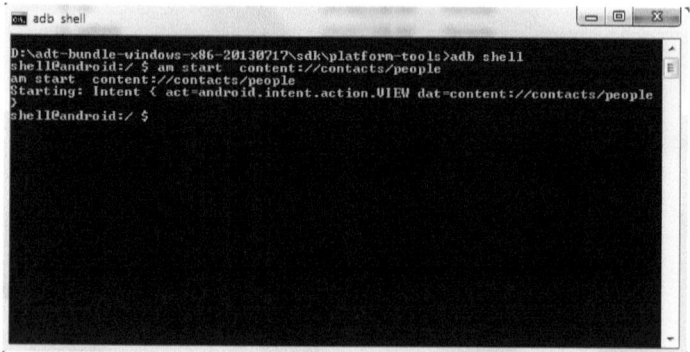

And output of this command is below.

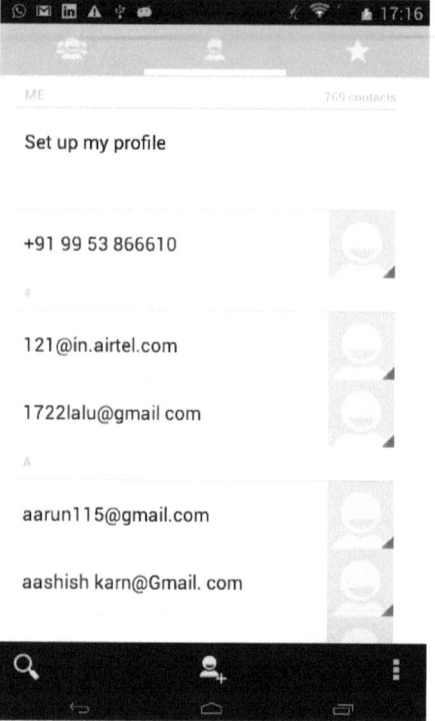

And we can add or create a contact using start command.

**Ex:am start -a android.intent.action.INSERT -t vnd.android.
cursor.dir/contact -e name 'Android Auto' -e phone 1234567890**

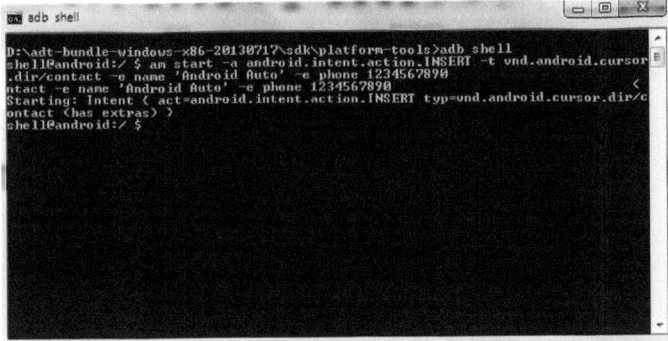

And output of the command is

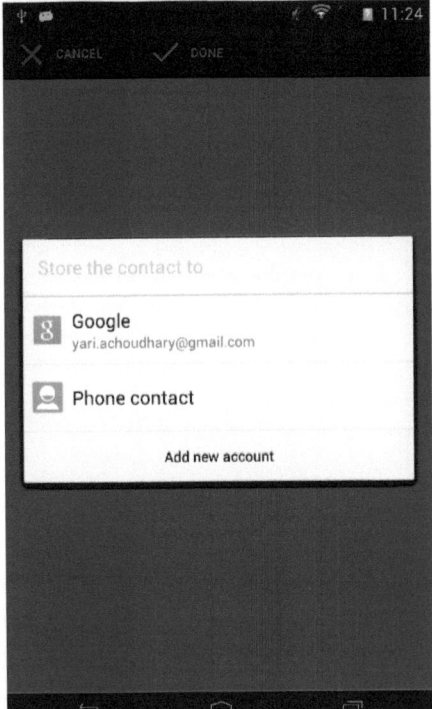

We can also make a call using start command.

Ex: am start -a android.intent.action.CALL -d tel:777

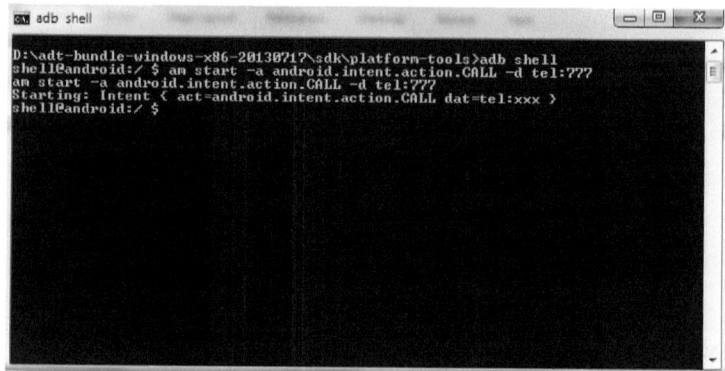

And out of the this command is

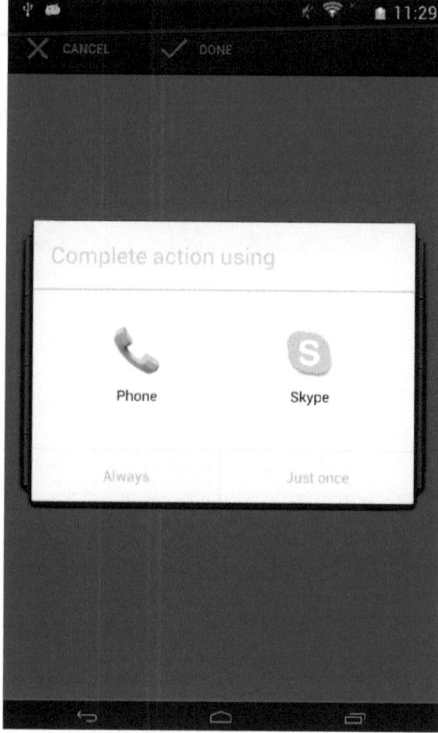

- **Start Service command**

From this command we can start ant device service.

Ex: am startservice –n <package name>/.<service name>

Or
am startservice<Intent>

- **Kill package command**

Kill package command use to kill whole package including all activity and service. This command kill all process in a package in safe mode and do not affect other processes.

Ex: am kill <package name>

58 | Android Firmware Customization

- **Kill all services command**

This command kills all background services and aped up your device and efficiency.

Ex: am kill-all

- **Broadcast command**

This command use to access our device any broadcast receiver class.

Ex: am broadcast <package name>/.<name of broadcast>

Or

am broadcast <Intent>

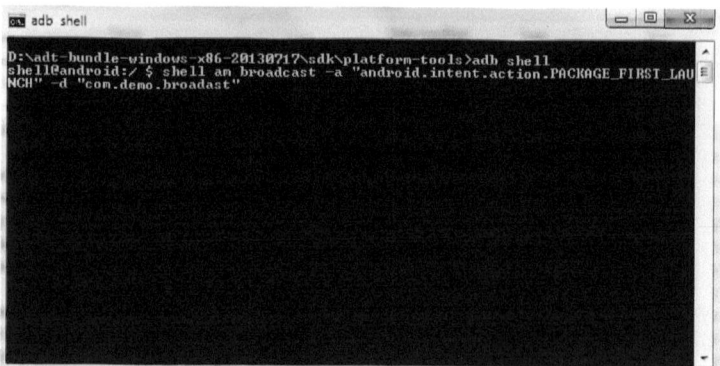

- **Force stop command**

Force stop command uses to force stop any package.

Ex: am force-stop <package name>

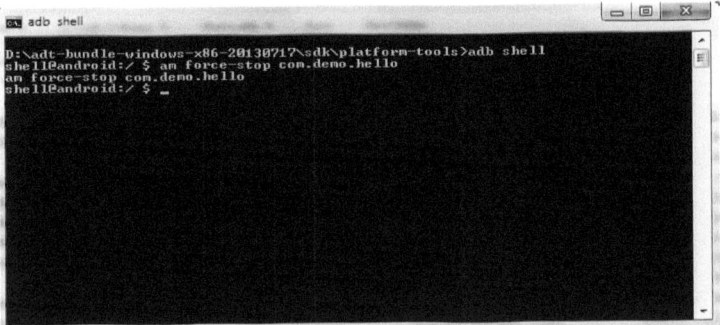

- **Instrument command**

Instrument commands use to start monitoring with an instrument instance. These commands use to testing purpose of device.

Ex: am instrument -w <test_package_name>/<runner_class>

And component of package in form <test_package>/<runner class>.am instrument -w <test_package_nwhere <test_package_name> is the Android package name of your test application, and <runner_class> is the name of the Android test runner class you are using

- w flag use to Forces an instrument to wait until the instrumentation terminates before terminating itself.

- r flag use to view result in raw format.

- e<TEST_OPTIONS> flags use Provides testing options as key-value pairs.

We can test a class in three types
- unit Tests
- function Tests
- Integration Tests

- **Debug app command**

We can debug android application using as command.

Ex: as set-debug-app <package name>

- **Clear debug app command**

Clear debug app command use to clear debug data in a package.

Ex: am clear-debug-app

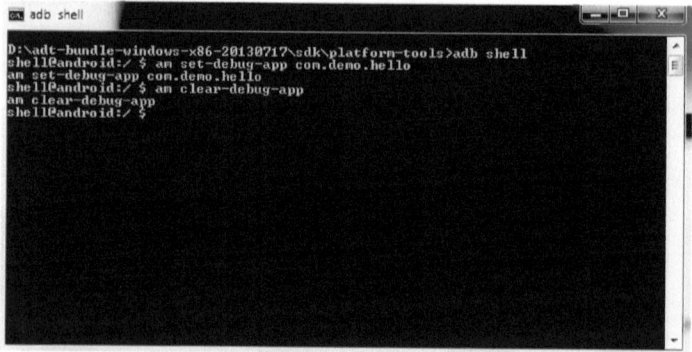

- **Monitor Command**

Some time we may got error in our program like unfortunately crash or ANR(application not responding)
    To check this command we use monitor command to resolve it.

Ex: am monitor [option]
- **Screen compact command**

In sometime we may need to adjust package screen compatibility to adjust screen resolution compatibility so we use this command for this purpose or we need to control screen resolution.

Ex: am screen-compat [on|off] <package name>

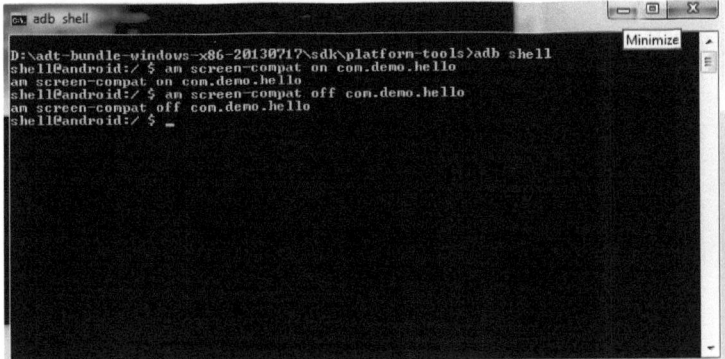

- **Change screen size**

This command use to adjust device screen size according to user requirement.

Ex: am display-size<screen size in pixel>

- **Change screen density**

This command change device screen display density.

Ex: am display-density<dpi>

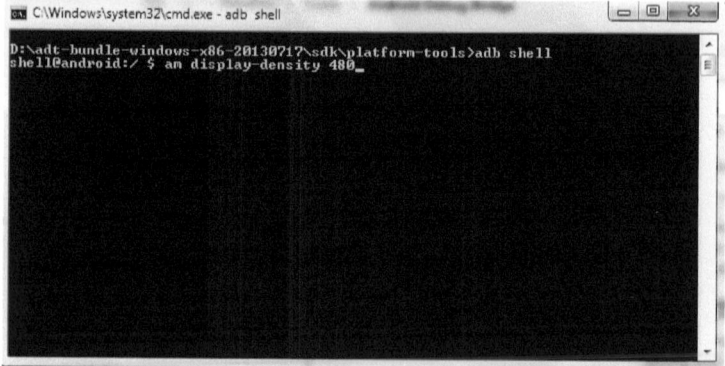

Unit 6: Package Manager Commands

In this chapter we will learn about different activity manger command. For this commands we can know all information about all or any device package applications.

- **What is Package Manager Commands**

Package manager (pm) command apply to all android package it may be system application or third party application packages. We can perform actions and queries on application packages installed on the device.

- **List package command**

This command use to view all android application packages in your device.

Ex: pm list package

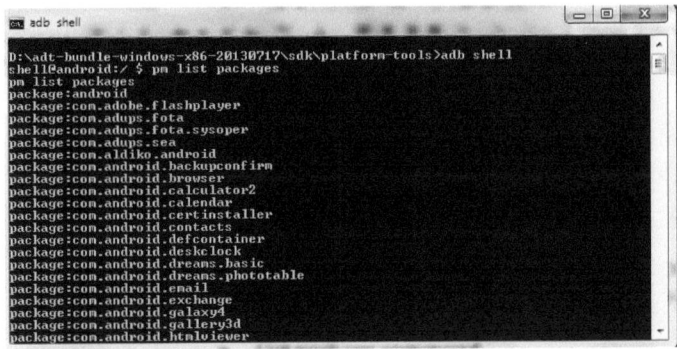

We can also filter list of packages.

Ex: aslist packages [options] <FILTER>
And types of filter
-f: view associated file.
-d: view disabled packages.
-e: view enabled packages.
-s: contain system packages.
-3: view third party packages.
-i: contain installer for the packages.
-u: include uninstalled packages.

- **List permission group command**

List permission group command use to show all group Permission which used for android application package in device just like camera, battery, network etc.

Ex: pm list permission-groups

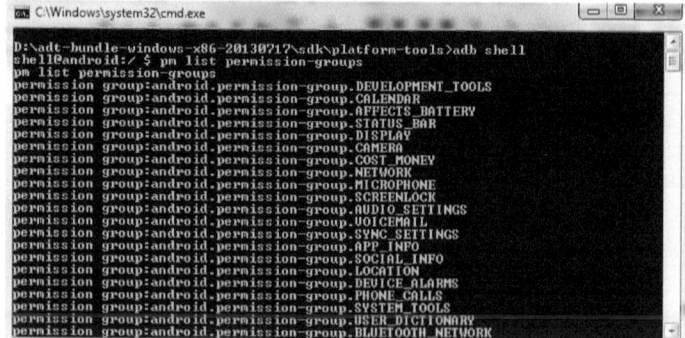

We can filter groups.

-g: Organize by group.

-f: Print all information.

-s: Short summary.

-d: Only list dangerous permissions.

-u: List only the permissions users will see.

Ex: pm list permissions [options] <GROUP>

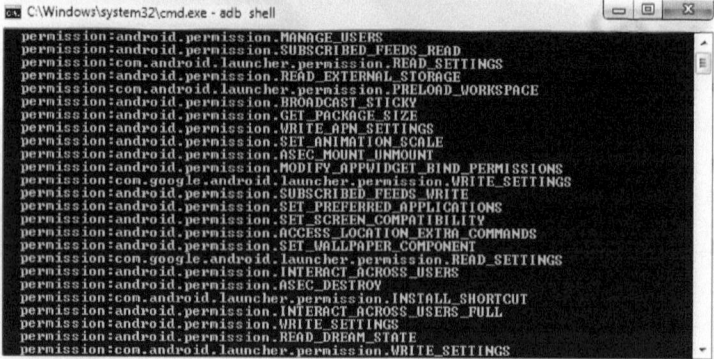

- **List instrumentation command**

This command shows list of all test packages.

Ex: pm list instrumentation –f

-f : Use for list of apk files.

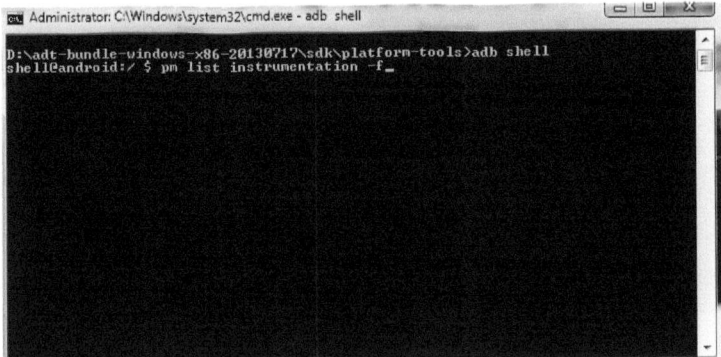

- **System features command**

It shows all features of device like just like camera, Bluetooth, network and map etc .

Ex: pm list features

- **List libraries**

This command use to show all android libraries in which are use in device currently.

Ex: pm list libraries

```
D:\adt-bundle-windows-x86-20130717\sdk\platform-tools>adb shell
shell@android:/ $ pm list libraries
pm list libraries
library:android.test.runner
library:com.android.future.usb.accessory
library:com.android.location.provider
library:com.google.android.maps
library:com.google.android.media.effects
library:com.google.widevine.software.drm
library:javax.obex
shell@android:/ $
```

- **List users**

This command show list of all users currently use in device.

Ex: pm list users

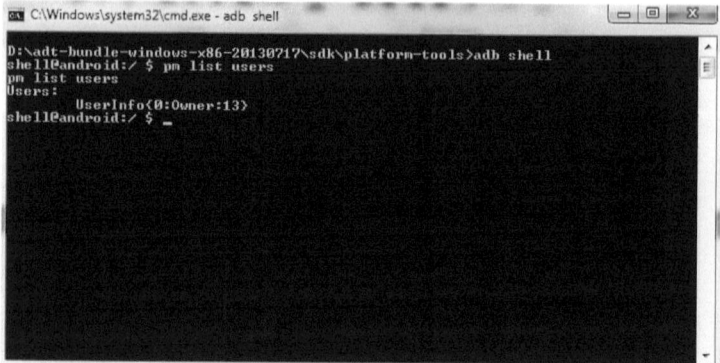

- **apk Path**

Through this command we can find apk full path in device.

Ex: pm path <package name>

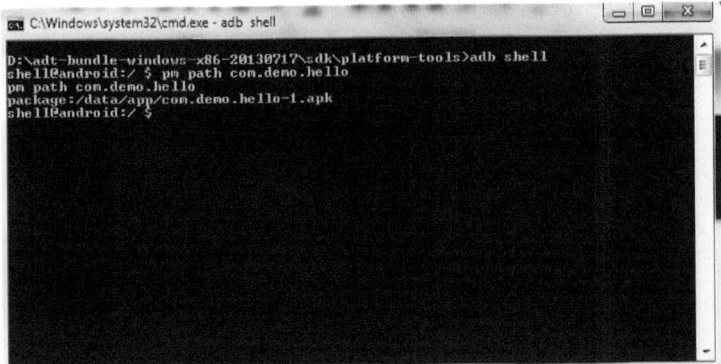

- **Install Application**

From this command we can install any apk in any specific location in our device.

Ex: pm install [option] <path>

There are many types of option for installation.
-r: Reinstall an existing app, keeping its data.
-t: Allow test APKs to be installed.
-i: Specify the installer package name.
-s: Install package on the shared mass storage (sdcard).
-f: Install package on the internal system memory.
-d: Allow version code downgrade.

- **Uninstall Application**

This command use to uninstall any application from device.

Ex: pm uninstall <package>

```
D:\adt-bundle-windows-x86-20130717\sdk\platform-tools>adb shell
shell@android:/ $ pm uninstall com.demo.hello
pm uninstall com.demo.hello
Success
shell@android:/ $
```

We can keep the data and cache directories using option

Ex: pm uninstall [option] <package>

```
D:\adt-bundle-windows-x86-20130717\sdk\platform-tools>adb shell
shell@android:/ $ pm uninstall -k com.demo.hello
pm uninstall -k com.demo.hello
Success
shell@android:/ $
```

- **Clear package**

This pm command use to clear all data associate with package.

Ex: pm clear <package name>

```
D:\adt-bundle-windows-x86-20130717\adt-bundle-windows-x86-20130717\sdk\platform-tools>adb shell
shell@android:/ $ pm clear com.exp.hello
pm clear com.exp.hello
Success
shell@android:/ $
```

- **Enable package component**

This pm command use to enable any package or component like class in your device.

Ex: pm enable <package or class name>

```
D:\adt-bundle-windows-x86-20130717\adt-bundle-windows-x86-20130717\sdk\platform-tools>adb shell
shell@android:/ $ pm enable com.exp.hello
pm enable com.exp.hello
Killed
137|shell@android:/ $
```

- **Disable package or component**

This pm command use to disable any package or component like class in your device.

Ex: pm disable <package or class name>

- **Grant permission**

This command use to provide user permission to package.

Ex: pm grant <package permission>

```
Microsoft Windows [Version 6.2.9200]
(c) 2012 Microsoft Corporation. Med ensamrätt.

C:\Users\Tobbe>adb shell
adb server is out of date.  killing...
* daemon started successfully *
shell@android:/ $ pm grant jp.co.c_lis.ccl.morelocale android.permission.CHANGE_CONFIGURATION
ocale android.permission.CHANGE_CONFIGURATION
shell@android:/ $
```

- **Set install location**

This command use to install any application on particular location

Ex:pmset-install-location <LOCATION>

We can install in three locations
0 [auto]-represented to system location
1 [internal]-represented to internal location
2 [external]-represented to system location

```
D:\adt-bundle-windows-x86-20130717\adt-bundle-windows-x86-20130717\sdk\platform-tools>adb shell
shell@android:/ $ pm set-install-location 0
pm set-install-location 0
shell@android:/ $ pm set-install-location 1
pm set-install-location 1
shell@android:/ $ pm set-install-location 2
pm set-install-location 2
shell@android:/ $
```

Unit 7: Screenshot and screen recoding

There are lots of new features in android. The main two important features, screenshot and screen recording are in android kit-kat. Screenshot available in all versions for android but screen recording feature is available on kit-kat or higher level versions.

- **Screenshot**

We can take screenshot in many types in android like with hard button, with android adb command android programming and it is save in screenshot directory in sdcard. To take screenshot with hard button we will have to press and hold home power and volume button at same time.

Screen shot file in android device located in /system/bin directory.

In below picture we can see screencap and screenshot files in device.

Name	Date modified	Type	Size
s62xd	7/22/2015 4:33 PM	File	26 KB
sbchk	7/22/2015 4:33 PM	File	74 KB
schedtest	7/22/2015 4:33 PM	File	6 KB
schedtop	7/22/2015 4:33 PM	System file	1 KB
screencap	7/22/2015 4:33 PM	File	10 KB
screenshot	7/22/2015 4:33 PM	File	38 KB
sdcard	7/22/2015 4:33 PM	File	14 KB
sdiotool	7/22/2015 4:33 PM	File	6 KB
send_bug	7/22/2015 4:33 PM	File	1 KB
sendevent	7/22/2015 4:33 PM	System file	1 KB
sensorservice	7/22/2015 4:33 PM	File	6 KB
service	7/22/2015 4:33 PM	File	14 KB
servicemanager	7/22/2015 4:33 PM	File	10 KB
setconsole	7/22/2015 4:33 PM	System file	1 KB
setprop	7/22/2015 4:33 PM	System file	1 KB
settings	7/22/2015 4:33 PM	File	1 KB
sh	7/22/2015 4:33 PM	System file	1 KB
shutdown	7/22/2015 4:33 PM	File	10 KB
sleep	7/22/2015 4:33 PM	System file	1 KB
smd	7/22/2015 4:33 PM	System file	1 KB

- **Screenshot with adb command**

We can take screenshot with adb command.

Ex: adb shell screencap –p <path to storage>

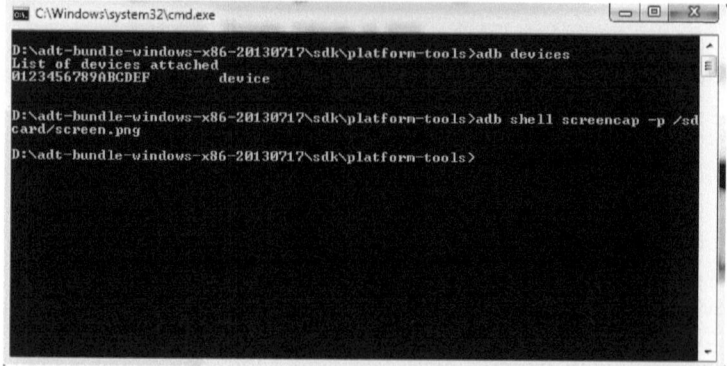

We can pull this screenshot image

Ex: adb pull/sdcard/screen.png

We can also delete this screen shot using this command

Ex: adb shell rm /sdcard/screen.png

- **Screen Recording**

There are lots of improvements done in kikat and one of the features is screen recording. Screen recording is the shell command use to record device screen in video presentation form. We get screen record achieved in form of MPEG. Screen recording feature available in kitkat (API level 19) or higher version.

Ex: adb shell screenrecord <path of file>

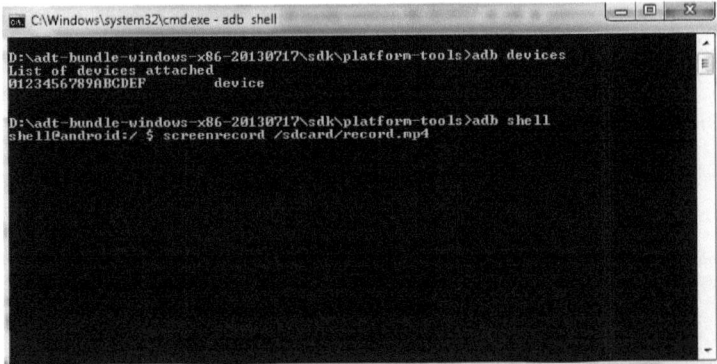

We can stop screen recording by press ctrl+c otherwise recording will be stop in 3 minute automatically.

There are some limitations of screen recording.
1. in some screen recording may be not work in high resolution device so always use low resolution device for screen recording.
2. screen rotations does not support by screen recording.
3. audio does not support.

- **Set size of screen recording**

We can set size of screen but default screen size is 1280*780.

Ex: screenrecord size<width*height> /sdcard/screen.mp4

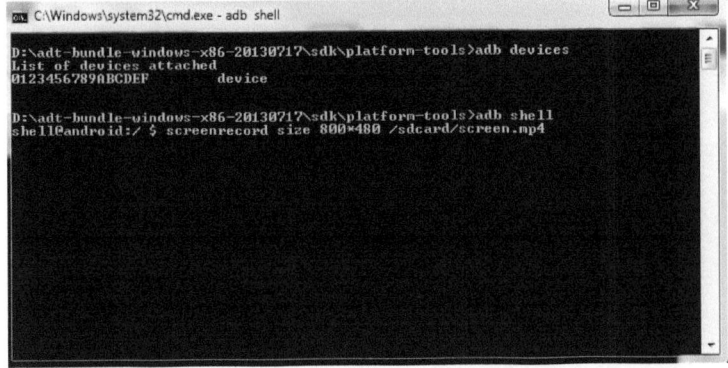

- **Set bit rate of screen recoding**

As well as we can set bit rate of screen recording. Bit rate of screen record is set in form of megabit per second and the default value is 4Mbps.

Bit rate=1/video quality

It means if we increase bit rate then video quality will be decrease.

Ex: screenrecord --bit-rate<rate> /sdcard/screen.mp4

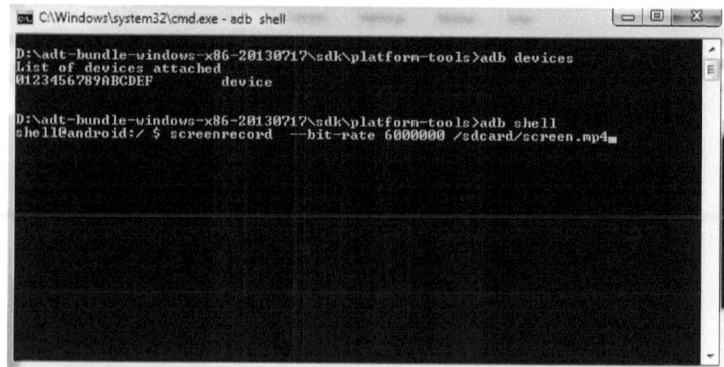

- **Set time limit of screen recording**

As well we can also set time limit of screen recording. The recording time is set in form of second and the default time is 180(3 second).

Ex: screenrecord --time-limit<time> /sdcard/screen.mp4

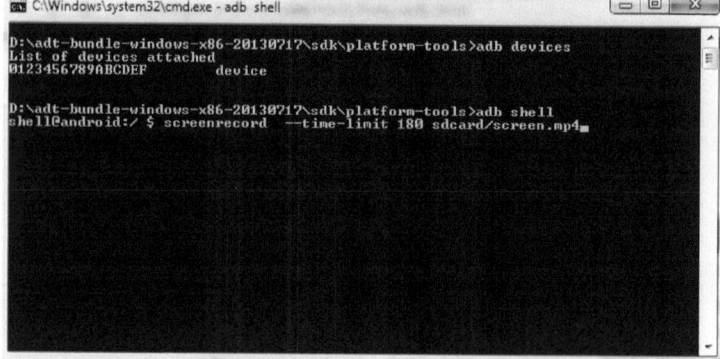

- **Set rotation of screen recording**

We can also set screen rotation of recording

Ex: screenrecord --rotation <degree> /sdcard/record.mp4

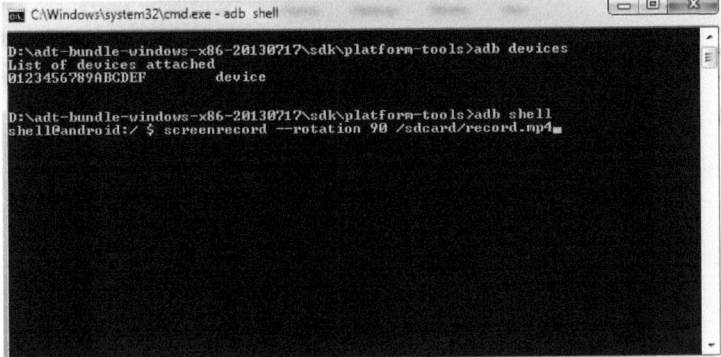

- **Verbose**

Verbose display log information on display .if you does not set any option in command utility does not display any information

Ex: screenrecord –verbose /sdcard/screen.mp4

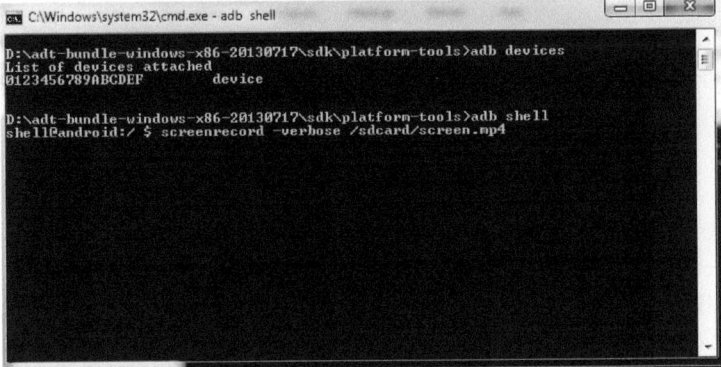

Unit 8: Other command

There are lots of other commands in android like monkey testing, sql database commands, logcat commands and server commands.

- **UI/Application Exerciser Monkey command**

This is also shell command use to testing purpose of any device and application or in other word we can say that use to debug app or device. This application test system event like click, volume, touch, gestures.

Ex: adb shell monkey –v -p <app package name> 500

Where v is verbosity and p represent package name.

- **Sqlite database command**

With sqlite database command we can manage a database which creates by an application. There are lots of adb commands like .dump which show output of the table and .schema create a table.

Ex: adb shell sqlite3 data/data/<package name>/database/<database name>

- **Other adb Commands**

1) **Restart usb:**
   Adb usb restart usb mode.
   Ex: adb usb

2) **List of device**
   We can show all device which attached with usb.
   Ex: adb devices

3) **Restart host**
   We can start host with adb commands.
   Ex: adb tcpip 5555

- **Other shell Commands**

All shell programs is located in bin directory in system directory and help of this program we can run all commands.

Ex: adb shell ls /system/bin

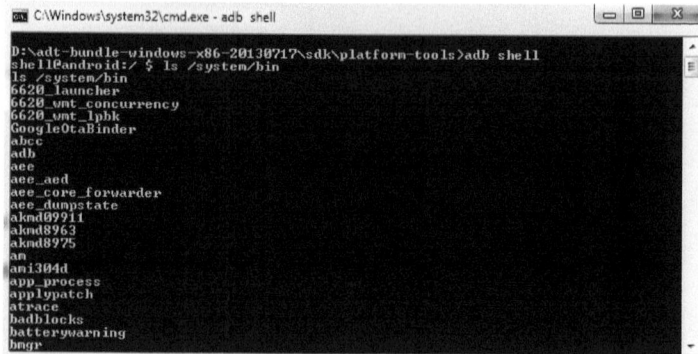

You can see in picture there are lots of programs.
1) dumpsys
2) dumpstate
3) dmesg
4) start
5) stop

Unit 9: dumpsys Commands

Dumpsys is tool to get various information form android device and show to user, this means we can find device information by dumpsys program and these commands also use for testing of android device.

- **EMEI No/phone Information**

We can find device EMEI number and device id of any device.

Ex: adb shell dumpsys iphonesubinfo

```
D:\adt-bundle-windows-x86-20130717\sdk\platform-tools>adb shell dumpsys iphonesu
binfo
Phone Subscriber Info:
    Phone Type = GSM
    Device ID = 911245950025964

D:\adt-bundle-windows-x86-20130717\sdk\platform-tools>_
```

- **Device battery**

We can find information about device battery from this program like battery manufacture name and status and the other information.

Ex: adb shell dumpsys battery

```
D:\adt-bundle-windows-x86-20130717\sdk\platform-tools>adb shell
shell@android:/ $ dumpsys battery
dumpsys battery
Current Battery Service state:
  AC powered: false
  USB powered: true
  Wireless powered: false
  status: 2
  health: 2
  present: true
  level: 34
  scale: 100
  voltage:3818
  temperature: -200
  technology: Li-ion
shell@android:/ $
```

- **WIFI**

Form this command we can view all information about device wifi like wifi name, wifi address and other information .

Ex: adb shell dumpsys wifi

```
C:\Windows\system32\cmd.exe - adb shell
Configured networks
* ID: 0 SSID: "W-11_2d24" BSSID: null PRIO: 17
  KeyMgmt: NONE Protocols: WPA RSN
  AuthAlgorithms:
  PairwiseCiphers: TKIP CCMP
  GroupCiphers: WEP40 WEP104 TKIP CCMP
  PSK:
  eap:
  phase2:
  identity:
  anonymous_identity:
  password:
  client_cert:
  engine: 0
  engine_id:
  key_id:
  ca_cert:
  ca_cert2:
IP assignment: UNASSIGNED
Proxy settings: UNASSIGNED
InterfaceName: wlan0 LinkAddresses: [192.168.169.23/24,] Routes: [0.0.0.0/0 -> 1
92.168.169.1,] DnsAddresses: [192.168.169.1,]
  imsi: null simSlot: null pcsc: null
Channel: 0 ChannelWidth: 1
```

- **CPU**

Form this prom we can also show all information about device CPU.

Ex: adb shell dumpsys cpuinfo

```
C:\Windows\system32\cmd.exe - adb shell
D:\adt-bundle-windows-x86-20130717\sdk\platform-tools>adb shell
shell@android:/ $ dumpsys cpuinfo
dumpsys cpuinfo
Load: 6.15 / 6.33 / 6.55
CPU usage from 44620ms to 39606ms ago:
  17% 791/com.zte.mobile.MushroomDay: 14% user + 2.9% kernel / faults: 120 minor
  12% 52/disp_config_upd: 0% user + 12% kernel
  7.9% 133/surfaceflinger: 5.5% user + 2.3% kernel / faults: 106 minor
  1.9% 550/system_server: 0.9% user + 0.9% kernel / faults: 32 minor
  1.7% 718/com.android.systemui: 1.3% user + 0.3% kernel / faults: 35 minor
  0.9% 985/com.google.process.gapps: 0.5% user + 0.3% kernel / faults: 119 minor
2 major
  0.9% 11400/kworker/0:2: 0% user + 0.9% kernel
  0.5% 45/bat_thread_kthr: 0% user + 0.5% kernel
  0.5% 11307/kworker/u:0: 0% user + 0.5% kernel
  0.1% 53/mmcqd/0: 0% user + 0.1% kernel
  0% 674/tx_thread: 0% user + 0% kernel
  0.1% 779/com.android.phone: 0.1% user + 0% kernel
  0.1% 10870/com.facebook.katana: 0.1% user + 0% kernel / faults: 3 minor
26% TOTAL: 13% user + 12% kernel + 0.1% iowait + 0.3% softirq
shell@android:/ $
```

- **Location**

This dumpsys program show about your device current location.

Ex: adb shell dumpsys location

```
D:\adt-bundle-windows-x86-20130717\sdk\platform-tools>adb shell
shell@android:/ $ dumpsys location
dumpsys location
Current Location Manager state:
  Location Listeners:
    Reciever[416ab348 listener UpdateRecord[passive com.google.android.gms(10012
> Request[POWER_NONE passive fastest=0]]]
    Reciever[41829b50 listener UpdateRecord[passive com.google.android.gms(10012
> Request[POWER_NONE passive fastest=0]]]
    Reciever[418374d8 listener UpdateRecord[passive android(1000) Request[POWER_
NONE passive fastest=0]]]
    Reciever[4177a560 listener UpdateRecord[passive android(1000) Request[POWER_
NONE passive fastest=0]]]
  Records by Provider:
    passive:
      UpdateRecord[passive android(1000) Request[POWER_NONE passive fastest=0]]
      UpdateRecord[passive android(1000) Request[POWER_NONE passive fastest=0]]
      UpdateRecord[passive com.google.android.gms(10012) Request[POWER_NONE pass
ive fastest=0]]
      UpdateRecord[passive com.google.android.gms(10012) Request[POWER_NONE pass
ive fastest=0]]
  Last Known Locations:
  Geofences:
  Enabled Providers:
```

- **Disk Memory**

This command provide information about disk space like total disk space, cache space, available space.

Ex: adb shell dumpsys diskstats

```
D:\adt-bundle-windows-x86-20130717\sdk\platform-tools>adb shell
shell@android:/ $ dumpsys diskstats
dumpsys diskstats
Latency: 0ms [512B Data Write]
Data-Free: 634580K / 1335720K total = 47% free
Cache-Free: 371440K / 378208K total = 98% free
System-Free: 224476K / 655984K total = 34% free
shell@android:/ $
```

- **Network**

This command provides full information about your device network.

Ex: adb shell dumpsys netstat

```
D:\adt-bundle-windows-x86-20130717\sdk\platform-tools>adb shell
shell@android:/ $ dumpsys netstat
dumpsys netstat
Can't find service: netstat
shell@android:/ $
```

- **Provider**

This command provide information about our device content provider full information like phone contact information or message or whatapp contact information.

Ex: adb shell dumpsys telephony.registry

```
D:\adt-bundle-windows-x86-20130717\sdk\platform-tools>adb shell
shell@android:/ $ dumpsys telephony.registry
dumpsys telephony.registry
last known state:
  mCallState=0
  mCallIncomingNumber=
  mServiceState=SIM1 0 home Airtel 40410 40410  HSPA CSS not supported -1 -1 Roa
mInd=-1 DefRoamInd=-1 EmergOnly=false Regist state: 1
  mSignalStrength=SignalStrength:SIM1 18 -1 -120 -160 -120 -1 -1 99 2147483647 2
147483647 2147483647 2147483647 gsm|lte -220 -274 -54
  mMessageWaiting=false
  mCallForwarding=false
  mDataActivity=0
  mDataConnectionState=-1
  mDataConnectionPossible=true
  mDataConnectionReason=nwTypeChanged
  mDataConnectionApn=
  mDataConnectionLinkProperties=null
  mDataConnectionLinkCapabilities=null
  mCellLocation=Bundle[mParcelledData.dataSize=104]
  mCellInfo=null
registrations: count=19
  KeyguardUpdateMonitor 0x1
  AudioService 0x20
```

- **User Permission**

This command provides information about all permission which use by in all applications in device.

```
adb shell
        android.permission.GET_TASKS
        android.permission.WRITE_EXTERNAL_STORAGE
        com.android.vending.billing.ADD_CREDIT_CARD
        com.google.android.googleapps.permission.GOOGLE_AUTH.cp
        com.google.android.gms.permission.ACTIVITY_RECOGNITION
        android.permission.WRITE_GSERVICES
        android.permission.BROADCAST_STICKY
        com.google.android.providers.settings.permission.WRITE_GSETTINGS
        android.permission.UPDATE_DEVICE_STATS
        com.android.vending.INTENT_VENDING_ONLY
        android.permission.NFC
        android.permission.WRITE_PROFILE
        android.permission.CHANGE_WIFI_STATE
        com.google.android.googleapps.permission.ACCESS_GOOGLE_PASSWORD
        android.permission.VIBRATE
        android.permission.READ_CALL_LOG
        android.permission.SUBSCRIBED_FEEDS_WRITE
SharedUser [android.uid.phone] (41f7ef00):
    userId=1001 gids=[3002, 3001, 3003, 1006, 1015, 1028, 1004, 2002]
    grantedPermissions:
        android.permission.MASTER_CLEAR
        android.permission.CLEAR_APP_USER_DATA
        android.permission.WRITE_CALL_LOG
        android.permission.SHUTDOWN
        android.permission.CALL_PHONE
```

- **Process and PID**

This command provides all information about all processes and all process ids about of device.

Ex: adb shell dumpsys meminfo

```
C:\Windows\system32\cmd.exe - adb shell
D:\adt-bundle-windows-x86-20130717\sdk\platform-tools>adb shell
shell@android:/ $ dumpsys meminfo
dumpsys meminfo
Applications Memory Usage (kB):
Uptime: 21708510 Realtime: 34056754

Total PSS by process:
    53052 kB: com.whatsapp (pid 12090)
    29914 kB: com.google.android.gm (pid 12937)
    28868 kB: com.facebook.katana (pid 16450)
    28378 kB: system (pid 545)
    26643 kB: com.linkedin.android (pid 12812)
    16552 kB: com.google.android.gms (pid 1731)
    14807 kB: android.process.acore (pid 16358)
    14741 kB: com.android.systemui (pid 657)
    14547 kB: com.android.launcher (pid 782)
    12991 kB: com.zte.mobile.MushroomDay (pid 722)
    12867 kB: com.google.process.gapps (pid 980)
    12169 kB: com.google.android.gms.persistent (pid 999)
    11370 kB: com.android.inputmethod.latin (pid 748)
    10178 kB: com.android.phone (pid 736)
     9826 kB: com.android.settings (pid 16034)
     6541 kB: com.google.android.apps.maps (pid 2444)
     4805 kB: android.process.media (pid 16016)
```

- **Account**

This command provide all information about all account of device like Google account or other application account like whatapp account link dean account and yahoo account.

84 | Android Firmware Customization

Ex: adb shell dumpsys account

```
C:\Windows\system32\cmd.exe - adb shell

D:\adt-bundle-windows-x86-20130717\sdk\platform-tools>adb shell
shell@android:/ $ dumpsys account
dumpsys account
User UserInfo{0:Owner:13}:
  Accounts: 4
    Account {name=y...        ...on, type=com.google}
    Account {name=t...  ...    ...in, type=com.google}
    Account {name=WhatsApp, type=com.whatsapp}
    Account {name=trainings@infoland.co.in, type=com.linkedin.android}

  Active Sessions: 0

  RegisteredServicesCache: 7 services
    ServiceInfo: AuthenticatorDescription {type=com.skype.contacts.sync}, Component
Info{com.skype.raider/com.skype.android.service.AccountService}, uid 10074
    ServiceInfo: AuthenticatorDescription {type=com.android.exchange}, Component
Info{com.android.email/com.android.email.service.EasAuthenticatorService}, uid 1
0019
    ServiceInfo: AuthenticatorDescription {type=com.android.email}, ComponentInf
o{com.android.email/com.android.email.service.PopImapAuthenticatorService}, uid
10019
    ServiceInfo: AuthenticatorDescription {type=com.linkedin.android}, Component
Info{com.linkedin.android/com.linkedin.android.authenticator.AuthenticationServi
ce}, uid 10076
```

- **Activities**

This command provides all information about all activities use in device like that app name, app package name, activates and provider as well as service.

Ex: adb dumpsys activity

```
C:\Windows\system32\cmd.exe - adb shell

AppStateContentProvider>
    proc=ProcessRecord{426969c0 1731:com.google.android.gms/u0a10012}
    authority=com.google.android.gms.appstate
  * ContentProviderRecord{422f82e0 u0 com.google.android.gsf/.talk.TalkProvider}
    proc=ProcessRecord{422d71f8 980:com.google.android.process.gapps/u0a10012}
    authority=com.google.android.providers.talk
  * ContentProviderRecord{4268b888 u0 com.google.android.apps.maps/com.google.go
oglenav.provider.NavigationAvailabilityProvider}>
    proc=ProcessRecord{426c9198 2444:com.google.android.apps.maps/u0a10040}
    authority=com.google.android.maps.NavigationAvailabilityProvider
  * ContentProviderRecord{42532fb8 u0 com.facebook.katana/.generated_content_pro
viders.com.facebook.katana.provider.UserStatusesProvider}>
    proc=ProcessRecord{425cf388 17019:com.facebook.katana/u0a10071}
    authority=com.facebook.katana.provider.UserStatusesProvider
  * ContentProviderRecord{427dd630 u0 com.android.providers.contacts/.ContactsPr
ovider2}
    proc=ProcessRecord{41ebd638 16358:android.process.acore/u0a10003}
    launchingApp=ProcessRecord{41ebd638 16358:android.process.acore/u0a10003}
    authority=com.android.contacts;com.android.contacts
  * ContentProviderRecord{42682160 u0 com.google.android.gms/.people.debug.Peopl
eExportProvider}
    proc=ProcessRecord{426969c0 1731:com.google.android.gms/u0a10012}
    authority=com.google.android.gms.people.export
  * ContentProviderRecord{4256d3f0 u0 com.facebook.katana/com.facebook.prefs.mul
```

- **Window**

This dumpsys command use to show window display information like keyboard and z order.

Ex: adb shell dumpsys window

```
mCur=(0,29)-(480,768)
mContent=(0,29)-(480,768)
mDock=(0,29)-(480,768)
mDockLayer=268435456 mStatusBarLayer=151000
mShowingLockscreen=false mShowingDream=false mDreamingLockscreen=false
mStatusBar=Window{426304d0 u0 StatusBar}
mNavigationBar=Window{424c5e60 u0 NavigationBar}
mKeyguard=Window{42086440 u0 Keyguard}
mFocusedWindow=Window{426304d0 u0 StatusBar}
mTopFullscreenOpaqueWindowState=Window{426704b8 u0 com.android.launcher/com.
android.launcher2.Launcher}
mTopIsFullscreen=false mHideLockScreen=false
mForceStatusBar=false mForceStatusBarFromKeyguard=false
mDismissKeyguard=0 mWinDismissingKeyguard=null mHomePressed=false
mAllowLockscreenWhenOn=false mLockScreenTimeout=60000 mLockScreenTimerActive
=false
mEndcallBehavior=2 mIncallPowerBehavior=1 mLongPressOnHomeBehavior=-1
mLandscapeRotation=1 mSeascapeRotation=3
mPortraitRotation=0 mUpsideDownRotation=2
mHdmiRotation=1 mHdmiRotationLock=true
mDockMode=0 mCarDockRotation=-1 mDeskDockRotation=-1
mUserRotationMode=0 mUserRotation=0 mAllowAllRotations=1
mCurrentAppOrientation=-1
mCarDockEnablesAccelerometer=true mDeskDockEnablesAccelerometer=true
mLidKeyboardAccessibility=0 mLidNavigationAccessibility=0 mLidControlsSleep=
```

- **Alarm**

This command use to show all information about alarm and alarm intents.

Ex: adb shell dumpsys alarm

```
mCur=(0,29)-(480,768)
mContent=(0,29)-(480,768)
mDock=(0,29)-(480,768)
mDockLayer=268435456 mStatusBarLayer=151000
mShowingLockscreen=false mShowingDream=false mDreamingLockscreen=false
mStatusBar=Window{426304d0 u0 StatusBar}
mNavigationBar=Window{424c5e60 u0 NavigationBar}
mKeyguard=Window{42086440 u0 Keyguard}
mFocusedWindow=Window{426304d0 u0 StatusBar}
mTopFullscreenOpaqueWindowState=Window{426704b8 u0 com.android.launcher/com.
android.launcher2.Launcher}
mTopIsFullscreen=false mHideLockScreen=false
mForceStatusBar=false mForceStatusBarFromKeyguard=false
mDismissKeyguard=0 mWinDismissingKeyguard=null mHomePressed=false
mAllowLockscreenWhenOn=false mLockScreenTimeout=60000 mLockScreenTimerActive
=false
mEndcallBehavior=2 mIncallPowerBehavior=1 mLongPressOnHomeBehavior=-1
mLandscapeRotation=1 mSeascapeRotation=3
mPortraitRotation=0 mUpsideDownRotation=2
mHdmiRotation=1 mHdmiRotationLock=true
mDockMode=0 mCarDockRotation=-1 mDeskDockRotation=-1
mUserRotationMode=0 mUserRotation=0 mAllowAllRotations=1
mCurrentAppOrientation=-1
mCarDockEnablesAccelerometer=true mDeskDockEnablesAccelerometer=true
mLidKeyboardAccessibility=0 mLidNavigationAccessibility=0 mLidControlsSleep=
```

- **GFX**

This command shows all information about gfx use in device just like OpenGL lib and classes.

- **Surface Flinger**

This command shows all information about Graphics of your device.

- **Storage Manager**

Ex: adb shell dumpsys devicestoragemonitor

This command also shows storage manager like internal, external and cache memory.

Unit 9: dumpsys Commands | 87

[screenshot: adb shell dumpsys devicestoragemonitor output]

- **Network Management**

This command shows all information about device network management.

Ex: adb shell dumpsys network_management

[screenshot: adb shell dumpsys network_management output]

- **Notification**

This command show all information about all notification received to device.

Ex: adb shell dumpsys notification

```
D:\adt-bundle-windows-x86-20130717\sdk\platform-tools>adb shell
shell@android:/ $ dumpsys notification
dumpsys notification
Current Notification Manager state:
  Notification List:
    NotificationRecord(42472c00 pkg=android id=20500ea tag=null score=0)
      icon=0x1080543 / android:drawable/stat_sys_data_usb
      pri=0
      score=0
      contentIntent=PendingIntent{4250bce8: PendingIntentRecord{4250bc90 android startActivity}}
      deleteIntent=null
      tickerText=Connected as USB Storage
      contentView=android.widget.RemoteViews@4250aef8
      uid=1000 userId=-1
      defaults=0x0
      flags=0x2
      sound=null
      vibrate=null
      ledARGB=0x0 ledOnMS=0 ledOffMS=0
    NotificationRecord(422ec558 pkg=android id=1040450 tag=null score=-10)
      icon=0x1080525 / android:drawable/stat_sys_adb
      pri=-1
      score=-10
```

- **Application Widget**

This command provides full information about all application widget.

Ex: adb shell dumpsys appwidget

```
D:\adt-bundle-windows-x86-20130717\sdk\platform-tools>adb shell
shell@android:/ $ dumpsys appwidget
dumpsys appwidget
User: 0
  Providers:
    [0] provider com.android.browser/.widget.BookmarkThumbnailWidgetProvider:
      min=(46081x28161)    minResize=(28161x10241) updatePeriodMillis=0 resizeMod
e=31 autoAdvanceViewId=-1 initialLayout=#7f04000e uid=10007 zombie=false
    [1] provider com.android.calendar/.widget.CalendarAppWidgetProvider:
      min=(28161x46081)    minResize=(28161x28161) updatePeriodMillis=0 resizeMod
e=33 autoAdvanceViewId=-1 initialLayout=#7f04000e uid=10009 zombie=false
    [2] provider com.android.contacts/.socialwidget.SocialWidgetProvider:
      min=(66561x10241)    minResize=(66561x10241) updatePeriodMillis=86400000 re
sizeMode=01 autoAdvanceViewId=-1 initialLayout=#7f0400c0 uid=10003 zombie=false
    [3] provider com.android.deskclock/com.android.alarmclock.AnalogAppWidgetPro
vider:
      min=(28161x28161)    minResize=(28161x28161) updatePeriodMillis=0 resizeMod
e=01 autoAdvanceViewId=-1 initialLayout=#7f040008 uid=10017 zombie=false
    [4] provider com.android.deskclock/com.android.alarmclock.DigitalAppWidgetPr
ovider:
      min=(40961x17921)    minResize=(40961x17921) updatePeriodMillis=0 resizeMod
e=33 autoAdvanceViewId=-1 initialLayout=#7f040016 uid=10017 zombie=false
    [5] provider com.android.email/.provider.WidgetProvider:
      min=(46081x28161)    minResize=(46081x28161) updatePeriodMillis=0 resizeMod
```

- **Audio**

This command provides information about audio like audio recorder, audio player, audio types, and audio volume.

Ex: adb shell dumpsys audio

```
C:\Windows\system32\cmd.exe - adb shell

D:\adt-bundle-windows-x86-20130717\sdk\platform-tools>adb shell
shell@android:/ $ dumpsys audio
dumpsys audio
Audio Focus stack entries:

Remote Control stack entries:
    pi: PendingIntent<42134ad8: PendingIntentRecord<41c70cd0 android broadcastInte
nt>> -- pack: null  -- ercvr: ComponentInfo<com.android.music/com.android.music.
MediaButtonIntentReceiver>  -- client: null  -- uid: -1  -- type: 0  state: 1

Remote Control Client stack entries:
    uid: -1  -- id: 1  -- type: 0  -- state: 1  -- vol handling: 1  -- vol: 15  --
volMax: 15  -- volObs: null

Remote Volume State:
    has remote: false
    is remote active: false
    rccId: -1
    volume handling: PLAYBACK_VOLUME_VARIABLE(1)
    volume: 13
    volume steps: 13
Stream volumes (device: index)
```

- **Backup**

This command provide information about system backup like last back information, backup size, which applications use for backup.

Ex: adb shell dumpsys backup

```
C:\Windows\system32\cmd.exe

D:\adt-bundle-windows-x86-20130717\sdk\platform-tools>adb shell
shell@android:/ $ dumpsys backup
dumpsys backup
Backup Manager is enabled / provisioned / not pending init
Auto-restore is enabled
Last backup pass started: 1434608908114 (now = 1434611550558)
    next scheduled: 1434612508114
Available transports:
  * com.google.android.backup/.BackupTransportService
    destination: yari.achoudhary@gmail.com
    intent: Intent ( act=com.google.android.backup.SetBackupAccountActivity )

    @pm@ - 344 state bytes
    com.android.calendar - 100 state bytes
    com.google.android.googlequicksearchbox - 32 state bytes
    com.android.browser - 0 state bytes
    com.android.providers.settings - 52 state bytes
    android - 100 state bytes
    com.android.vending - 0 state bytes
    com.android.providers.userdictionary - 8 state bytes
    com.android.inputmethod.latin - 112 state bytes
    com.android.sharedstoragebackup - 0 state bytes
    com.google.android.gm - 8 state bytes
android/com.android.internal.backup.LocalTransport
```

- **Clipboard**

This command provides information about clipboard like clipboard manager.

Ex: adb shell dumpsys clipboard

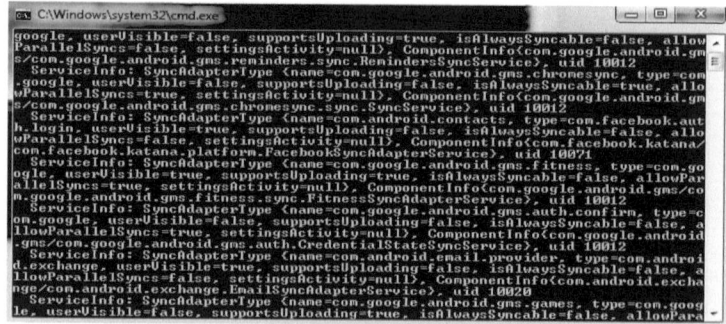

- **Content**

Content class show the data so this command display full description about content manager classes use in android device.

Ex: adb shell dumpsys content

- **Input Method**

This command provides information about input method like keyboard and other input in android device.

Ex: adb shell dumpsys input_mehtod

```
D:\adt-bundle-windows-x86-20130717\sdk\platform-tools>adb shell
shell@android:/ $ dumpsys input_method
dumpsys input_method
Current Input Method Manager state:
  Input Methods:
  InputMethod #0:
    mId=com.android.inputmethod.latin/.LatinIME mSettingsActivityName=com.androi
d.inputmethod.latin.SettingsActivity
    mIsDefaultResId=0x7f090000
    Service:
      priority=0 preferredOrder=0 match=0x108000 specificIndex=-1 isDefault=fals
e
      ServiceInfo:
        name=com.android.inputmethod.latin.LatinIME
        packageName=com.android.inputmethod.latin
        labelRes=0x7f0b002e nonLocalizedLabel=null icon=0x0
        enabled=true exported=true processName=com.android.inputmethod.latin
        permission=android.permission.BIND_INPUT_METHOD
        flags=0x0
  InputMethod #1:
    mId=com.google.android.googlequicksearchbox/com.google.android.voicesearch.i
me.VoiceInputMethodService mSettingsActivityName=com.google.android.voicesearch.
VoiceSearchPreferences
    mIsDefaultResId=0x0
```

- **Camera**

This command explains about device camera and camera application which use to camera and other information just like camera quality.

Ex: adb shell dumpsys media.camera

```
D:\adt-bundle-windows-x86-20130717\sdk\platform-tools>adb shell
shell@android:/ $ dumpsys media.camera
dumpsys media.camera
Camera module HAL API version: 0x0
Camera module API version: 0x1
Camera module name: MTK Camera Module
Camera module author: MTK
Number of camera devices: 3

Camera 0 static information:
  Facing: BACK
  Orientation: 90
  Device version: 0x100
  Device is closed, no client instance
Camera 1 static information:
  Facing: FRONT
  Orientation: 270
  Device version: 0x100
  Device is closed, no client instance
Camera 2 static information:
  Facing: BACK
  Orientation: 0
  Device version: 0x100
  Device is closed, no client instance
```

- **Storage**

This command explains about storage method of device just like that storage type, storage path, storage partition and other information.

Ex: adb shell dumpsys mount

- **Player**

This command provides information about media player just like audio recording and other media player classes.

Ex: adb shell dumpsys media.player

- **Power**

This command provides information about power management just like power conception, power management classes.

Ex: adb shell dumpsys power

```
C:\Windows\system32\cmd.exe - adb shell
D:\adt-bundle-windows-x86-20130717\sdk\platform-tools>adb shell
shell@android:/ $ dumpsys power
dumpsys power
POWER MANAGER (dumpsys power)

Power Manager State:
  mDirty=0x0
  mWakefulness=Awake
  mIsPowered=true
  mPlugType=2
  mBatteryLevel=72
  mBatteryLevelWhenDreamStarted=0
  mDockState=0
  mStayOn=true
  mProximityPositive=false
  mBootCompleted=true
  mSystemReady=true
  mWakeLockSummary=0x0
  mUserActivitySummary=0x0
  mRequestWaitForNegativeProximity=false
  mSandmanScheduled=false
  mLastWakeTime=2716304 (79781 ms ago)
  mLastSleepTime=2669589 (126496 ms ago)
  mSendWakeUpFinishedNotificationWhenReady=false
```

- **Search**

This command provides information about search application and search classes.

Ex: adb shell dumpsys search

```
C:\Windows\system32\cmd.exe - adb shell
D:\adt-bundle-windows-x86-20130717\sdk\platform-tools>adb shell
shell@android:/ $ dumpsys search
dumpsys search
User: 0
  Searchable authorities:
    applications
    browser
    browser
    com.android.contacts
    call_log
    com.mediatek.email.provider.EmailSuggestionsProvider
    media
    com.google.android.maps.SuggestionProvider
    com.google.android.maps.SuggestionProvider
    com.google.android.maps.SuggestionProvider
    com.google.android.maps.SuggestionProvider
    com.google.android.maps.SuggestionProvider
    com.android.mms.SuggestionsProvider
    media
    com.google.android.finsky.RecentSuggestionsProvider
    com.google.android.finsky.RecentSuggestionsProvider
    com.google.android.finsky.QSBSuggestionsProvider2
```

- **Sensor**

This command full explains about sensors just like accelerometer and sensor services.

Ex: adb shell dumpsys sensorservice

```
D:\adt-bundle-windows-x86-20130717\sdk\platform-tools>adb shell
shell@android:/ $ dumpsys sensorservice
dumpsys sensorservice
Sensor List:
KXTJ2-1009 3-axis Accelerometer         | Kionix
   | 0x00000000 | maxRate=  0.00Hz | last=< 0.0, 0.0, 0.0>
9-axis fusion disabled (0 clients), gyro-rate=  0.00Hz, q=< 0, 0, 0, 0 > (0), b
=< 0, 0, 0 >
1 h/w sensors:
handle=0x00000000, active-count=1, rates(ms)=< 66.7 >, selected=66.7 ms
1 active connections
Active sensors:
KXTJ2-1009 3-axis Accelerometer  (handle=0x00000000, connections=1)
shell@android:/ $
```

- **Status Bar**

This command provides describe about status bar like icon list, status bar notification.

Ex: adb shell dumpsys starusbar

```
D:\adt-bundle-windows-x86-20130717\sdk\platform-tools>adb shell
shell@android:/ $ dumpsys statusbar
dumpsys statusbar
Icon list:
   0: (ime) null
   1: (sync_failing) StatusBarIcon(pkg=com.android.systemuiuser=0 id=0x7f020208
level=0 visible=false num=0 )
   2: (sync_active) StatusBarIcon(pkg=com.android.systemuiuser=0 id=0x7f020207 l
evel=0 visible=false num=0 )
   3: (gps) null
   4: (bluetooth) StatusBarIcon(pkg=com.android.systemuiuser=0 id=0x7f02014e lev
el=0 visible=false num=0 )
   5: (nfc) null
   6: (headset) StatusBarIcon(pkg=com.android.systemuiuser=0 id=0x7f0201df level
=0 visible=false num=0 )
   7: (tty) StatusBarIcon(pkg=com.android.systemuiuser=0 id=0x7f020209 level=0 v
isible=false num=0 )
   8: (speakerphone) null
   9: (mute) null
  10: (volume) StatusBarIcon(pkg=com.android.systemuiuser=0 id=0x7f0201e2 level=
0 visible=false num=0 )
  11: (wifi) null
  12: (cdma_eri) StatusBarIcon(pkg=com.android.systemuiuser=0 id=0x7f0201e4 leve
l=0 visible=false num=0 )
```

- **Gesture**

This command provides information about gesture application and gesture classes.

Ex: adb shell dumpsys gesture

```
com.india.ambraneindia.MainActivity: 2 starts, 750-1000ms=1, 2000-3000ms=1
com.india.ambraneindia.HomeActivity: 2 starts, 0-250ms=1, 750-1000ms=1
com.android.launcher: 31 times, 9516342 ms
   com.android.launcher2.Launcher: 31 starts, 2000-3000ms=1, 4000-5000ms=1, >=5000ms=2
com.android.gallery3d: 6 times, 764982 ms
   com.android.gallery3d.app.Gallery: 16 starts, 250-500ms=2
   com.android.gallery3d.gadget.WidgetTypeChooser: 2 starts, 0-250ms=2
   com.android.camera.CameraLauncher: 2 starts, 500-750ms=1, 1000-1500ms=1
   com.android.gallery3d.app.MovieActivity: 14 starts, 0-250ms=1, 250-500ms=12, 500-750ms=1
   com.android.gallery3d.gadget.WidgetConfigure: 5 starts, 250-500ms=5
   com.android.gallery3d.app.AlbumPicker: 1 starts, 250-500ms=1
com.android.settings: 2 times, 41556 ms
   com.android.settings.Settings: 4 starts, 1000-1500ms=1, 2000-3000ms=1
   com.android.settings.SubSettings: 2 starts, 250-500ms=1, 1000-1500ms=1
com.whatsapp: 15 times, 7006675 ms
   com.whatsapp.Conversation: 43 starts, 500-750ms=11, 750-1000ms=11, 1000-1500ms=8, 1500-2000ms=5, 2000-3000ms=1, 4000-5000ms=1
   com.whatsapp.HomeActivity: 43 starts, 750-1000ms=2, 1000-1500ms=6, 1500-2000ms=3, 2000-3000ms=1, 4000-5000ms=1
   com.whatsapp.Main: 2 starts
   com.whatsapp.GroupChatInfo: 4 starts, 750-1000ms=1, 1000-1500ms=2, 2000-3000ms=1
   com.whatsapp.MediaView: 3 starts, 250-500ms=3
```

- **Wallpaper**

This command provide information about wallpaper just like wallpaper classes and wallpaper services.

Ex: adb shell dumpsys wallpaper

```
D:\adt-bundle-windows-x86-20130717\sdk\platform-tools>adb shell
shell@android:/ $ dumpsys wallpaper
dumpsys wallpaper
Current Wallpaper Service state:
 User 0:
  mWidth=838 mHeight=800
  mName=
  mWallpaperComponent=ComponentInfo{com.zte.mobile.MushroomDay/com.zte.mobile.MushroomDay.WallpaperServiceMushroom}
  Wallpaper connection com.android.server.WallpaperManagerService$WallpaperConnection@42a6a1d0:
    mInfo.component=ComponentInfo{com.zte.mobile.MushroomDay/com.zte.mobile.MushroomDay.WallpaperServiceMushroom}
    mToken=android.os.Binder@42a6a230
    mService=android.service.wallpaper.IWallpaperService$Stub$Proxy@425ea7f0
    mEngine=android.service.wallpaper.IWallpaperEngine$Stub$Proxy@425e06d0
    mLastDiedTime=-4803830
shell@android:/ $
```

Unit 10: Key Layout

In this chapter we will learn about key layout, key layout structure, storage location, types of key layout and description about keys.

- **Key Layout**

Key layouts are files in format of .kl which use to run key event by Linux device. There are no of specific predefined key used in android device like home, back, menu and other keys. There are two types of keys in android one is hard button keys and other is soft button keys.

- **Key Layout storage Location**

Around all key layout files are located in key layout folder which path is **/system/user/keylayout/** and some files are may be located in **/data/system/device/keylayout/** folder in android device.

You can understand better with picture.

The main file of key layout is genric.kl which content all key of keyboard and joystick.

- **Key Declaration**

There is a each key has specific role and perform specific action when press it in android device and each key assign a specific role just like that key 102 will be refer to home button so each key has some specific reason to use.

Some files are using some specific sentence. There is some sentences use with some key.

WAKE: wake mean that this key use when device will be wake or screen will be in on mode.

WAKE_DROPED: wake mean that this key use when device will be wake or screen will be in off mode.

SHIF: use for shift.

CAPS_LOCK: use for Capital Letter.

ALT: use for alt key press.

ALT_GR: use for right alt key press.

FUNCTION: use for function key press.

VIRTUAL: use for soft key press.

MENU: use for menu key.

- **Keyboard Keys**

There are lots of keyboard key. It may be hard code key or soft key just like that home Manu back because some kind of device may be contain hard code button or not.

key 1 ESCAPE
key 2 1
key 3 2
key 4 3
key 5 4
key 6 5
key 7 6
key 8 7
key 9 8
key 10 9
key 11 0
key 12 MINUS
key 13 EQUALS

```
key 14 DEL
key 15 TAB
key 16 Q
key 17 W
key 18 E
key 19 R
key 20 T
key 21 Y
key 22 U
key 23 I
key 24 O
key 25 P
key 26 LEFT_BRACKET
key 27 RIGHT_BRACKET
key 28 ENTER
key 29 CTRL_LEFT
key 30 A
key 31 S
key 32 D
key 33 F
key 34 G
key 35 H
key 36 J
key 37 K
key 38 L
key 39 SEMICOLON
key 40 APOSTROPHE
key 41 GRAVE
key 42 SHIFT_LEFT
key 43 BACKSLASH
key 44 Z
key 45 X
key 46 C
key 47 V
key 48 B
key 49 N
key 50 M
key 51 COMMA
key 52 PERIOD
key 53 SLASH
key 54 SHIFT_RIGHT
```

```
key 55 NUMPAD_MULTIPLY
key 56 ALT_LEFT
key 57 SPACE
key 58 CAPS_LOCK
key 59 F1
key 60 F2
key 61 F3
key 62 F4
key 63 F5
key 64 F6
key 65 F7
key 66 F8
key 67 F9
key 68 F10
key 69 NUM_LOCK
key 70 SCROLL_LOCK
key 71 NUMPAD_7
key 72 NUMPAD_8
key 73 NUMPAD_9
key 74 NUMPAD_SUBTRACT
key 75 NUMPAD_4
key 76 NUMPAD_5
key 77 NUMPAD_6
key 78 NUMPAD_ADD
key 79 NUMPAD_1
key 80 NUMPAD_2
key 81 NUMPAD_3
key 82 NUMPAD_0
key 83 NUMPAD_DOT
# key 84 (undefined)
key 85 ZENKAKU_HANKAKU
key 86 BACKSLASH
key 87 F11
key 88 F12
key 89 RO
# key 90 "KEY_KATAKANA"
# key 91 "KEY_HIRAGANA"
key 92 HENKAN
key 93 KATAKANA_HIRAGANA
key 94 MUHENKAN
key 95 NUMPAD_COMMA
```

```
key 96 NUMPAD_ENTER
key 97 CTRL_RIGHT
key 98 NUMPAD_DIVIDE
key 99 SYSRQ
key 100 ALT_RIGHT
# key 101 "KEY_LINEFEED"
key 102 MOVE_HOME
key 103 DPAD_UP
key 104 PAGE_UP
key 105 DPAD_LEFT
key 106 DPAD_RIGHT
key 107 MOVE_END
key 108 DPAD_DOWN
key 109 PAGE_DOWN
key 110 INSERT
key 111 FORWARD_DEL
# key 112 "KEY_MACRO"
key 113 VOLUME_MUTE
key 114 VOLUME_DOWN
key 115 VOLUME_UP
key 116 POWER WAKE
key 117 NUMPAD_EQUALS
# key 118 "KEY_KPPLUSMINUS"
key 119 BREAK
# key 120 (undefined)
key 121 NUMPAD_COMMA
key 122 KANA
key 123 EISU
key 124 YEN
key 125 META_LEFT
key 126 META_RIGHT
key 127 MENU WAKE_DROPPED
key 128 MEDIA_STOP
# key 129 "KEY_AGAIN"
# key 130 "KEY_PROPS"
# key 131 "KEY_UNDO"
# key 132 "KEY_FRONT"
# key 133 "KEY_COPY"
# key 134 "KEY_OPEN"
# key 135 "KEY_PASTE"
# key 136 "KEY_FIND"
```

```
# key 137 "KEY_CUT"
# key 138 "KEY_HELP"
key 139 MENU WAKE_DROPPED
key 140 CALCULATOR
# key 141 "KEY_SETUP"
key 142 POWER WAKE
key 143 POWER WAKE
# key 144 "KEY_FILE"
# key 145 "KEY_SENDFILE"
# key 146 "KEY_DELETEFILE"
# key 147 "KEY_XFER"
# key 148 "KEY_PROG1"
# key 149 "KEY_PROG2"
key 150 EXPLORER
# key 151 "KEY_MSDOS"
key 152 POWER WAKE
# key 153 "KEY_DIRECTION"
# key 154 "KEY_CYCLEWINDOWS"
key 155 ENVELOPE
key 156 BOOKMARK
# key 157 "KEY_COMPUTER"
key 158 BACK WAKE_DROPPED
key 159 FORWARD
key 160 MEDIA_CLOSE
key 161 MEDIA_EJECT
key 162 MEDIA_EJECT
key 163 MEDIA_NEXT
key 164 MEDIA_PLAY_PAUSE
key 165 MEDIA_PREVIOUS
key 166 MEDIA_STOP
key 167 MEDIA_RECORD
key 168 MEDIA_REWIND
key 169 CALL
# key 170 "KEY_ISO"
key 171 MUSIC
key 172 HOME
# key 173 "KEY_REFRESH"
# key 174 "KEY_EXIT"
# key 175 "KEY_MOVE"
# key 176 "KEY_EDIT"
key 177 PAGE_UP
```

```
key 178 PAGE_DOWN
key 179 NUMPAD_LEFT_PAREN
key 180 NUMPAD_RIGHT_PAREN
# key 181 "KEY_NEW"
# key 182 "KEY_REDO"
# key 183 F13
# key 184 F14
# key 185 F15
# key 186 F16
# key 187 F17
# key 188 F18
# key 189 F19
# key 190 F20
# key 191 F21
# key 192 F22
# key 193 F23
# key 194 F24
# key 195 (undefined)
# key 196 (undefined)
# key 197 (undefined)
# key 198 (undefined)
# key 199 (undefined)
key 200 MEDIA_PLAY
key 201 MEDIA_PAUSE
# key 202 "KEY_PROG3"
# key 203 "KEY_PROG4"
# key 204 (undefined)
# key 205 "KEY_SUSPEND"
# key 206 "KEY_CLOSE"
key 207 MEDIA_PLAY
key 208 MEDIA_FAST_FORWARD
# key 209 "KEY_BASSBOOST"
# key 210 "KEY_PRINT"
# key 211 "KEY_HP"
key 212 CAMERA
key 213 MUSIC
# key 214 "KEY_QUESTION"
key 215 ENVELOPE
# key 216 "KEY_CHAT"
key 217 SEARCH
# key 218 "KEY_CONNECT"
```

```
# key 219 "KEY_FINANCE"
# key 220 "KEY_SPORT"
# key 221 "KEY_SHOP"
# key 222 "KEY_ALTERASE"
# key 223 "KEY_CANCEL"
# key 224 "KEY_BRIGHTNESSDOWN"
# key 225 "KEY_BRIGHTNESSUP"
key 226 HEADSETHOOK

key 256 BUTTON_1
key 257 BUTTON_2
key 258 BUTTON_3
key 259 BUTTON_4
key 260 BUTTON_5
key 261 BUTTON_6
key 262 BUTTON_7
key 263 BUTTON_8
key 264 BUTTON_9
key 265 BUTTON_10
key 266 BUTTON_11
key 267 BUTTON_12
key 268 BUTTON_13
key 269 BUTTON_14
key 270 BUTTON_15
key 271 BUTTON_16

key 288 BUTTON_1
key 289 BUTTON_2
key 290 BUTTON_3
key 291 BUTTON_4
key 292 BUTTON_5
key 293 BUTTON_6
key 294 BUTTON_7
key 295 BUTTON_8
key 296 BUTTON_9
key 297 BUTTON_10
key 298 BUTTON_11
key 299 BUTTON_12
key 300 BUTTON_13
key 301 BUTTON_14
key 302 BUTTON_15
```

```
key 303 BUTTON_16

key 304 BUTTON_A
key 305 BUTTON_B
key 306 BUTTON_C
key 307 BUTTON_X
key 308 BUTTON_Y
key 309 BUTTON_Z
key 310 BUTTON_L1
key 311 BUTTON_R1
key 312 BUTTON_L2
key 313 BUTTON_R2
key 314 BUTTON_SELECT
key 315 BUTTON_START
key 316 BUTTON_MODE
key 317 BUTTON_THUMBL
key 318 BUTTON_THUMBR

# key 352 "KEY_OK"
key 353 DPAD_CENTER
# key 354 "KEY_GOTO"
# key 355 "KEY_CLEAR"
# key 356 "KEY_POWER2"
# key 357 "KEY_OPTION"
# key 358 "KEY_INFO"
# key 359 "KEY_TIME"
# key 360 "KEY_VENDOR"
# key 361 "KEY_ARCHIVE"
key 362 GUIDE
# key 363 "KEY_CHANNEL"
# key 364 "KEY_FAVORITES"
# key 365 "KEY_EPG"
key 366 DVR
# key 367 "KEY_MHP"
# key 368 "KEY_LANGUAGE"
# key 369 "KEY_TITLE"
# key 370 "KEY_SUBTITLE"
# key 371 "KEY_ANGLE"
# key 372 "KEY_ZOOM"
# key 373 "KEY_MODE"
# key 374 "KEY_KEYBOARD"
```

```
# key 375 "KEY_SCREEN"
# key 376 "KEY_PC"
key 377 TV
# key 378 "KEY_TV2"
# key 379 "KEY_VCR"
# key 380 "KEY_VCR2"
# key 381 "KEY_SAT"
# key 382 "KEY_SAT2"
# key 383 "KEY_CD"
# key 384 "KEY_TAPE"
# key 385 "KEY_RADIO"
# key 386 "KEY_TUNER"
# key 387 "KEY_PLAYER"
# key 388 "KEY_TEXT"
# key 389 "KEY_DVD"
# key 390 "KEY_AUX"
# key 391 "KEY_MP3"
# key 392 "KEY_AUDIO"
# key 393 "KEY_VIDEO"
# key 394 "KEY_DIRECTORY"
# key 395 "KEY_LIST"
# key 396 "KEY_MEMO"
key 397 CALENDAR
# key 398 "KEY_RED"
# key 399 "KEY_GREEN"
# key 400 "KEY_YELLOW"
# key 401 "KEY_BLUE"
key 402 CHANNEL_UP
key 403 CHANNEL_DOWN
# key 404 "KEY_FIRST"
# key 405 "KEY_LAST"
# key 406 "KEY_AB"
# key 407 "KEY_NEXT"
# key 408 "KEY_RESTART"
# key 409 "KEY_SLOW"
# key 410 "KEY_SHUFFLE"
# key 411 "KEY_BREAK"
# key 412 "KEY_PREVIOUS"
# key 413 "KEY_DIGITS"
# key 414 "KEY_TEEN"
# key 415 "KEY_TWEN"
```

key 429 CONTACTS

key 448 "KEY_DEL_EOL"
key 449 "KEY_DEL_EOS"
key 450 "KEY_INS_LINE"
key 451 "KEY_DEL_LINE"

key 464 FUNCTION
key 465 ESCAPE FUNCTION
key 466 F1 FUNCTION
key 467 F2 FUNCTION
key 468 F3 FUNCTION
key 469 F4 FUNCTION
key 470 F5 FUNCTION
key 471 F6 FUNCTION
key 472 F7 FUNCTION
key 473 F8 FUNCTION
key 474 F9 FUNCTION
key 475 F10 FUNCTION
key 476 F11 FUNCTION
key 477 F12 FUNCTION
key 478 1 FUNCTION
key 479 2 FUNCTION
key 480 D FUNCTION
key 481 E FUNCTION
key 482 F FUNCTION
key 483 S FUNCTION
key 484 B FUNCTION

key 497 KEY_BRL_DOT1
key 498 KEY_BRL_DOT2
key 499 KEY_BRL_DOT3
key 500 KEY_BRL_DOT4
key 501 KEY_BRL_DOT5
key 502 KEY_BRL_DOT6
key 503 KEY_BRL_DOT7
key 504 KEY_BRL_DOT8

- **Joystick Keys**

Joy stick key use for play games just like that screen axis.
axis 0x00 X
axis 0x01 Y
axis 0x02 Z
axis 0x03 RX
axis 0x04 RY
axis 0x05 RZ
axis 0x06 THROTTLE
axis 0x07 RUDDER
axis 0x08 WHEEL
axis 0x09 GAS
axis 0x0a BRAKE
axis 0x10 HAT_X
axis 0x11 HAT_Y

- **Input Key Event**

We have already discuss that in android each key has a specific role and each key assign number and with help of this number we can activate this button or press button but the main question is that how we can use this number to activate button so we have one option to use this number that we can use with help of adb command.

Ex: adb shell input keyevent <event code>

Here we are activating home button with help of adb shell command.

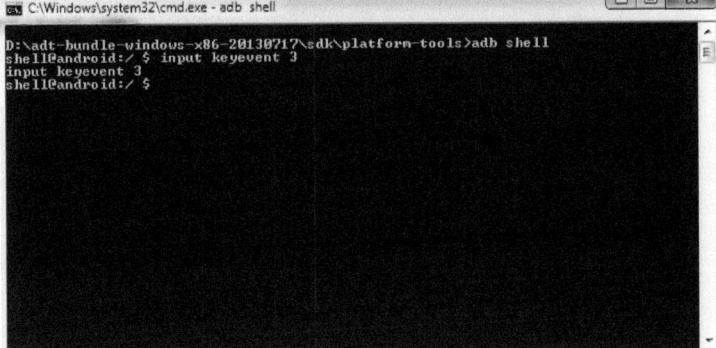

There some other key which you can see in below picture.

#	Keycode	#	Keycode
0	"KEYCODE_UNKNOWN"	43	"KEYCODE_O"
1	"KEYCODE_MENU"	44	"KEYCODE_P"
2	"KEYCODE_SOFT_RIGHT"	45	"KEYCODE_Q"
3	"KEYCODE_HOME"	46	"KEYCODE_R"
4	"KEYCODE_BACK"	47	"KEYCODE_S"
5	"KEYCODE_CALL"	48	"KEYCODE_T"
6	"KEYCODE_ENDCALL"	49	"KEYCODE_U"
7	"KEYCODE_0"	50	"KEYCODE_V"
8	"KEYCODE_1"	51	"KEYCODE_W"
9	"KEYCODE_2"	52	"KEYCODE_X"
10	"KEYCODE_3"	53	"KEYCODE_Y"
11	"KEYCODE_4"	54	"KEYCODE_Z"
12	"KEYCODE_5"	55	"KEYCODE_COMMA"
13	"KEYCODE_6"	56	"KEYCODE_PERIOD"
14	"KEYCODE_7"	57	"KEYCODE_ALT_LEFT"
15	"KEYCODE_8"	58	"KEYCODE_ALT_RIGHT"
16	"KEYCODE_9"	59	"KEYCODE_SHIFT_LEFT"
17	"KEYCODE_STAR"	60	"KEYCODE_SHIFT_RIGHT"
18	"KEYCODE_POUND"	61	"KEYCODE_TAB"
19	"KEYCODE_DPAD_UP"	62	"KEYCODE_SPACE"
20	"KEYCODE_DPAD_DOWN"	63	"KEYCODE_SYM"
21	"KEYCODE_DPAD_LEFT"	64	"KEYCODE_EXPLORER"
22	"KEYCODE_DPAD_RIGHT"	65	"KEYCODE_ENVELOPE"
23	"KEYCODE_DPAD_CENTER"	66	"KEYCODE_ENTER"
24	"KEYCODE_VOLUME_UP"	67	"KEYCODE_DEL"
25	"KEYCODE_VOLUME_DOWN"	68	"KEYCODE_GRAVE"
26	"KEYCODE_POWER"	69	"KEYCODE_MINUS"
27	"KEYCODE_CAMERA"	70	"KEYCODE_EQUALS"
28	"KEYCODE_CLEAR"	71	"KEYCODE_LEFT_BRACKET"
29	"KEYCODE_A"	72	"KEYCODE_RIGHT_BRACKET"
30	"KEYCODE_B"	73	"KEYCODE_BACKSLASH"
31	"KEYCODE_C"	74	"KEYCODE_SEMICOLON"
32	"KEYCODE_D"	75	"KEYCODE_APOSTROPHE"
33	"KEYCODE_E"	76	"KEYCODE_SLASH"
34	"KEYCODE_F"	77	"KEYCODE_AT"
35	"KEYCODE_G"	78	"KEYCODE_NUM"
36	"KEYCODE_H"	79	"KEYCODE_HEADSETHOOK"
37	"KEYCODE_I"	80	"KEYCODE_FOCUS"
38	"KEYCODE_J"	81	"KEYCODE_PLUS"
39	"KEYCODE_K"	82	"KEYCODE_MENU"
40	"KEYCODE_L"	83	"KEYCODE_NOTIFICATION"
41	"KEYCODE_M"	84	"KEYCODE_SEARCH"
42	"KEYCODE_N"	85	"TAG_LAST_KEYCODE"

Unit 11: Android Testing

In this chapter we will learn about testing, testing modules, android testing, types of testing and other information about testing

- **Android testing**

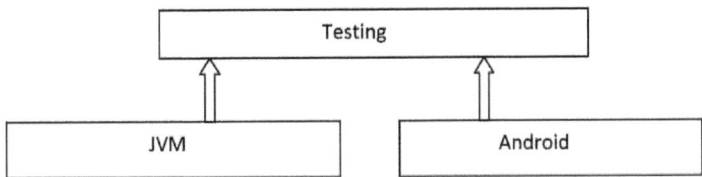

From above picture we can easily understand that testing contains with part one is JVM form java and other is android library.

- **Unit Testing**

In unit testing, test run on a local jvm on the development machine rather than android runtime.

Unit testing done by android.jar library, all exception methods include in android.jar and execute by default.

- **JUnit Testing**

You can use the JUnit TestCase class to do unit testing on a class that doesn't call Android APIs.

Testcase class is super class for androidTestCase. You can easily understand with given code.

```
Public class Testapp extends TestCase
{
Int a;
Int b;
}
Protectd void testMethod()
{
a=10;
b=10;
}
```

```
public void testMethod () {
int c = a + b;
 assertTrue(c == 5.0);
}
```

- **Monkey testing**

Monkey Talk is tools which use to test any android or I Phone application or test and device. In android SDK include these testing tools. We can test any device or any application with two types first JUnit testing and second is monkey testing. JUnit test any application by test classes and monkey is a command line tool which test with device action like touch screen, gesture and other.

- **Device Testing structure**

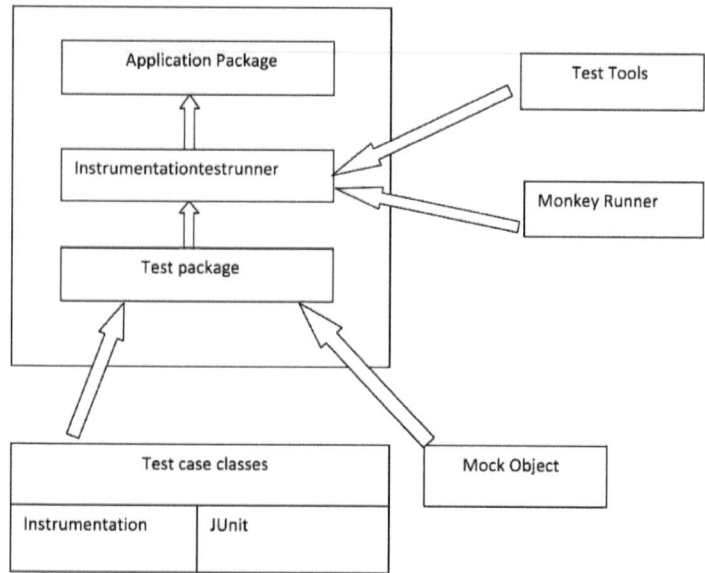

Monkey Testing Feature

There are four main feature of monkey testing.
- Basic configuration option
- Debugging option
- Event types
- Operational constraints

Unit 11: Android Testing | 111

- **Monkey Testing with Shell Command for device**

There are lot of a command to execute monkey testing.

Ex: adb shell monkey -v 500

Where –v represent verbose method and 500 is represent no. of event to be sent for testing.

```
D:\adt-bundle-windows-x86-20130717\sdk\platform-tools>adb shell monkey -v 500
* daemon not running. starting it now on port 5037 *
* daemon started successfully *
:Monkey: seed=1435901219663 count=500
:IncludeCategory: android.intent.category.LAUNCHER
:IncludeCategory: android.intent.category.MONKEY
// Event percentages:
//   0: 15.0%
//   1: 10.0%
//   2: 2.0%
//   3: 15.0%
//   4: -0.0%
//   5: 25.0%
//   6: 15.0%
//   7: 2.0%
//   8: 2.0%
//   9: 1.0%
//  10: 13.0%
:Switch: #Intent;action=android.intent.action.MAIN;category=android.intent.categ
ory.LAUNCHER;launchFlags=0x10200000;component=com.facebook.katana/.LoginActivity
;end
    // Allowing start of Intent { act=android.intent.action.MAIN cat=[android.in
tent.category.LAUNCHER] cmp=com.facebook.katana/.LoginActivity } in package com.
facebook.katana
```

- **Monkey Testing with Shell Command for application**

There are lots of commands to execute monkey testing.

Ex: adb shell monkey –p <package name> -v 500

Where -p represent package and –v represent verbose method and 500 is represent no. of event to be sent for testing.

```
D:\adt-bundle-windows-x86-20130717\sdk\platform-tools>adb shell
shell@android:/ $ monkey -p com.exp.hello -v 500
monkey -p com.exp.hello -v 500
:Monkey: seed=1435894521157 count=500
:AllowPackage: com.exp.hello
:IncludeCategory: android.intent.category.LAUNCHER
:IncludeCategory: android.intent.category.MONKEY
// Event percentages:
//   0: 15.0%
//   1: 10.0%
//   2: 2.0%
//   3: 15.0%
//   4: -0.0%
//   5: 25.0%
//   6: 15.0%
//   7: 2.0%
//   8: 2.0%
//   9: 1.0%
//  10: 13.0%
:Switch: #Intent;action=android.intent.action.MAIN;category=android.intent.categ
ory.LAUNCHER;launchFlags=0x10200000;component=com.exp.hello/.MainActivity;end
    // Allowing start of Intent { act=android.intent.action.MAIN cat=[android.in
tent.category.LAUNCHER] cmp=com.exp.hello/.MainActivity } in package com.exp.hel
lo
```

- **Run the same event sequence again in monkey testing**

Some time you want to check an application on same sequence or randomly again so you will have to test exact same sequence with monkey tool.

Ex: adb shell monkey –p <package name> -s 999 –v 500

Here –s refer to seed and 999 is seed value

- **Monkey testing with Event time**

If want to set fix time between events so we can do it by throttle.

Ex: adb shell monkey –p <package name>-- throttle 1000 –v 500

- **Monkey testing with Touch Event percentage**

We can also test an application touch event percentage.

Ex: adb shell monkey –p <package name>--pct-touch 25 –v 500

```
D:\adt-bundle-windows-x86-20130717\sdk\platform-tools>adb shell
shell@android:/ $ monkey -p com.demo --pct-touch 25 -v 500
monkey -p com.demo --pct-touch 25 -v 500
:Monkey: seed=1435891910448 count=500
:AllowPackage: com.demo
:IncludeCategory: android.intent.category.LAUNCHER
:IncludeCategory: android.intent.category.MONKEY
// Event percentages:
//   0: 25.0%
//   1: 8.823529%
//   2: 1.7647059%
//   3: 13.235294%
//   4: -0.0%
//   5: 22.058825%
//   6: 13.235294%
//   7: 1.7647059%
//   8: 1.7647059%
//   9: 0.88235295%
//  10: 11.470589%
:Switch: #Intent;action=android.intent.action.MAIN;category=android.intent.categ
ory.LAUNCHER;launchFlags=0x10200000;component=com.demo/.DatbaseActivity;end
    // Allowing start of Intent { act=android.intent.action.MAIN cat=[android.in
tent.category.LAUNCHER] cmp=com.demo/.DatbaseActivity } in package com.demo
:Sending Touch (ACTION_DOWN): 0:(89.0,652.0)
```

- **Monkey testing with Motion Event percentage**

We can also test an application motion event percentage.

Ex: adb shell monkey –p <package name>--pct-motion 25 –v 500

```
D:\adt-bundle-windows-x86-20130717\sdk\platform-tools>adb shell
shell@android:/ $ monkey -p com.demo --pct-motion 25 -v 500
monkey -p com.demo --pct-motion 25 -v 500
:Monkey: seed=1435893706549 count=500
:AllowPackage: com.demo
:IncludeCategory: android.intent.category.LAUNCHER
:IncludeCategory: android.intent.category.MONKEY
// Event percentages:
//   0: 12.5%
//   1: 25.0%
//   2: 1.6666666%
//   3: 12.5%
//   4: -0.0%
//   5: 20.833332%
//   6: 12.5%
//   7: 1.6666666%
//   8: 1.6666666%
//   9: 0.8333333%
//  10: 10.833333%
:Switch: #Intent;action=android.intent.action.MAIN;category=android.intent.categ
ory.LAUNCHER;launchFlags=0x10200000;component=com.demo/.DatbaseActivity;end
    // Allowing start of Intent { act=android.intent.action.MAIN cat=[android.in
tent.category.LAUNCHER] cmp=com.demo/.DatbaseActivity } in package com.demo
:Sending Touch (ACTION_DOWN): 0:(73.0,494.0)
```

114 | Android Firmware Customization

- **Monkey testing with Any Event percentage**

We can also test an application any event percentage.

Ex: adb shell monkey –p <package name>--pct-anyevent 25 –v 500

```
D:\adt-bundle-windows-x86-20130717\sdk\platform-tools>adb shell
shell@android:/ $ monkey -p com.demo --pct-anyevent 25 -v 500
monkey -p com.demo --pct-anyevent 25 -v 500
:Monkey: seed=1435889539614 count=500
:AllowPackage: com.demo
:IncludeCategory: android.intent.category.LAUNCHER
:IncludeCategory: android.intent.category.MONKEY
// Event percentages:
//   0: 12.931034%
//   1: 8.620689%
//   2: 1.7241379%
//   3: 12.931034%
//   4: -0.0%
//   5: 21.551723%
//   6: 12.931034%
//   7: 1.7241379%
//   8: 1.7241379%
//   9: 0.86206895%
//  10: 25.0%
:Switch: #Intent;action=android.intent.action.MAIN;category=android.intent.categ
ory.LAUNCHER;launchFlags=0x10200000;component=com.demo/.DatbaseActivity;end
    // Allowing start of Intent ( act=android.intent.action.MAIN cat=[android.in
tent.category.LAUNCHER] cmp=com.demo/.DatbaseActivity ) in package com.demo
:Sending Touch (ACTION_DOWN): 0:(37.0,153.0)
```

- **Monkey testing Number of Events**

We can also find no events use in any android device.

Ex: adb shell monkey --dbg-no-event –v 500

```
shell@android:/ $ monkey -p com.demo --dbg-no-events -v 500
monkey -p com.demo --dbg-no-events -v 500
:Monkey: seed=1435895578926 count=500
:AllowPackage: com.demo
:IncludeCategory: android.intent.category.LAUNCHER
:IncludeCategory: android.intent.category.MONKEY
// Event percentages:
//   0: 15.0%
//   1: 10.0%
//   2: 2.0%
//   3: 15.0%
//   4: -0.0%
//   5: 25.0%
//   6: 15.0%
//   7: 2.0%
//   8: 2.0%
//   9: 1.0%
//  10: 13.0%
Events injected: 500
:Sending rotation degree=0, persist=false
:Dropped: keys=0 pointers=0 trackballs=0 flips=0 rotations=0
## Network stats: elapsed time=157ms (0ms mobile, 157ms wifi, 0ms not connected)
// Monkey finished
shell@android:/ $
```

- **Monkey testing Ignore Crashes**

If we want fill full test an application without crashes we use this command or we want full test by avoid crashes. This Command avoids any type's exception.

Ex: adb shell monkey –p <package name> –ignore-crashes –v 500

```
D:\adt-bundle-windows-x86-20130717\sdk\platform-tools>adb shell
shell@android:/ $ monkey -p com.demo --ignore-crashes -v 500
monkey -p com.demo --ignore-crashes -v 500
:Monkey: seed=1436044805838 count=500
:AllowPackage: com.demo
:IncludeCategory: android.intent.category.LAUNCHER
:IncludeCategory: android.intent.category.MONKEY
// Event percentages:
//   0: 15.0%
//   1: 10.0%
//   2: 2.0%
//   3: 15.0%
//   4: -0.0%
//   5: 25.0%
//   6: 15.0%
//   7: 2.0%
//   8: 2.0%
//   9: 1.0%
//  10: 13.0%
:Switch: #Intent;action=android.intent.action.MAIN;category=android.intent.categ
ory.LAUNCHER;launchFlags=0x10200000;component=com.demo/.DatbaseActivity;end
    // Allowing start of Intent { act=android.intent.action.MAIN cat=[android.in
tent.category.LAUNCHER] cmp=com.demo/.DatbaseActivity } in package com.demo
:Sending Flip keyboardOpen=false
```

- **Monkey testing Ignore Timeouts**

If we want fill full test an application without time out exception we use this command or we want full test by avoid time out crashes.

Ex: adb shell monkey –p <package name> —ignore-timeouts –v 500

```
D:\adt-bundle-windows-x86-20130717\sdk\platform-tools>adb shell
shell@android:/ $ monkey -p com.demo --ignore-timeouts -v 500
monkey -p com.demo --ignore-timeouts -v 500
:Monkey: seed=1436045523750 count=500
:AllowPackage: com.demo
:IncludeCategory: android.intent.category.LAUNCHER
:IncludeCategory: android.intent.category.MONKEY
// Event percentages:
//   0: 15.0%
//   1: 10.0%
//   2: 2.0%
//   3: 15.0%
//   4: -0.0%
//   5: 25.0%
//   6: 15.0%
//   7: 2.0%
//   8: 2.0%
//   9: 1.0%
//  10: 13.0%
:Switch: #Intent;action=android.intent.action.MAIN;category=android.intent.categ
ory.LAUNCHER;launchFlags=0x10200000;component=com.demo/.DatbaseActivity;end
    // Allowing start of Intent { act=android.intent.action.MAIN cat=[android.in
tent.category.LAUNCHER] cmp=com.demo/.DatbaseActivity } in package com.demo
    // Rejecting start of Intent { act=android.intent.action.MAIN cat=[android.i
```

- **Monkey testing Ignore Security Exceptions**

If we want fill full test an application without security exception we use this command or we want full test by avoid security exception crashes.

Ex: adb shell monkey –p <package name> —ignore-security-excetions –v 500

```
C:\Windows\system32\cmd.exe - adb shell

D:\adt-bundle-windows-x86-20130717\sdk\platform-tools>adb shell
shell@android:/ $ monkey -p com.demo --ignore-security-exceptions -v 500
monkey -p com.demo --ignore-security-exceptions -v 500
:Monkey: seed=1436058308520 count=500
:AllowPackage: com.demo
:IncludeCategory: android.intent.category.LAUNCHER
:IncludeCategory: android.intent.category.MONKEY
// Event percentages:
//   0: 15.0%
//   1: 10.0%
//   2: 2.0%
//   3: 15.0%
//   4: -0.0%
//   5: 25.0%
//   6: 15.0%
//   7: 2.0%
//   8: 2.0%
//   9: 1.0%
//  10: 13.0%
:Switch: #Intent;action=android.intent.action.MAIN;category=android.intent.categ
ory.LAUNCHER;launchFlags=0x10200000;component=com.demo/.DatbaseActivity;end
    // Allowing start of Intent { act=android.intent.action.MAIN cat=[android.in
tent.category.LAUNCHER] cmp=com.demo/.DatbaseActivity } in package com.demo
:Sending Trackball (ACTION_MOVE): 0:(0.0,-5.0)
```

Unit 12: Android Rom and Structure

- **Android rom**

Rom is an operating system run on your device. It is store in read only memory in hardware segment where your firmware and all application store and all device come with a rom which install by manufacture. Android rom contains all flash files like system, boot and recovery. It is store in read only memory part on hardware.

- **Types of rom**

There are many android rom available in currently in market and mostly rom internal structure issame. We will discuss only few android rom but from help of this book you can customize around all rom. There are follow:
1) Stock rom
2) Rockchip rom
3) Mtk rom
4) Cyanogenmod rom

This rom is mostly currently most of manufacture use.

- **Custom rom**

Android is open source which allow developer to customize it and we can edit or update some new feature in it and build own new rom image for android phone or tablet or another word we can say that it is standard version of android operating system.

- **Advantage of custom rom**

These are some advantage of android custom rom:
1) Provide update version
2) Improve performance
3) Improve battery performance
4) Customize theme
5) Add some new feature

- **Disadvantage of custom rom**

These are some disadvantage of android custom rom.

1) Break manufactures warranty.

2) It may be defected rom

- **Android rom Structure**

There are mainly six partitions in android phone, tablet and other android device. In below are list of file systems. It may be exiting other file system it depend on android model but logically 6 partition in android devices.

1) **Boot**
   Boot file contain ramdisk and kernel.
2) **Recovery**
   It is provides advanced recovery, installation, restoration and maintenance operation for device.
3) **System**
   This partition contains the entire Android OS, other than the kernel and the ramdisk. This includes the Android GUI and all the system applications that come pre-installed on the device.
4) **Data**
   This partition contains the user's data like your contacts, sms, settings and all android applications that you have installed.
5) **Cache**
   This is the partition where Android stores accessed data and app components.
6) **Misc**
   This partition contains usb configuration and hardware setting etc.

Rom partition Structure					
Boot	System	Recovery	Data	Cache	Misc

And we can check system partition by df command

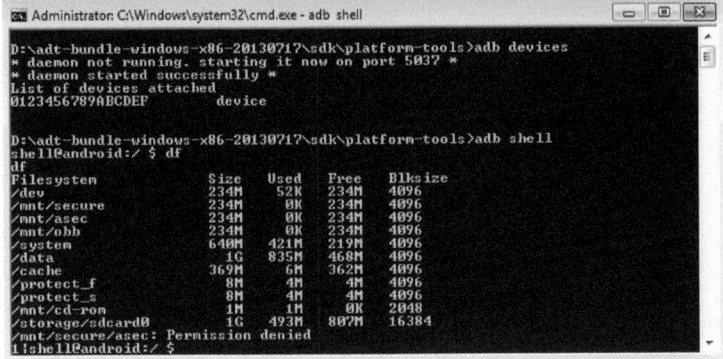

- **Stock Rom**

It is a cd Image file which builds in Linux operating system. This rom generally use in Chinese device like all winner devices.

Supported firmware images:

1) Sochip SC8600/SC9800
2) Boxchip F10/F15/F16/F20
3) Teclast T7200/T8100
4) Allwinner F10/F13/F18
5) Allwinner F1C100/F1E200
6) Allwinner A10/A13/A10s
7) Allwinner A20/A31/A31s
8) Allwinner A80 (Phoenix Suit)

You can see stock rom in below picture

Name	Date modified	Type	Size
stockrom.img	11/3/2014 6:58 PM	IMG File	831,591 KB

- **Structure and extract Stock Rom**

There lot of tools available in market to extract stock rom like imagere packer tools. When we extract this image file with imagere packer we will get many .fex files.

120 | Android Firmware Customization

Name	Date modified	Type	Size
imgrepacker	3/12/2014 12:34 PM	File	90 KB
imgRePacker.exe	3/12/2014 4:36 PM	Application	120 KB
imgRePacker.ini	3/20/2015 4:34 PM	Configuration sett...	1 KB
lzma.exe	4/4/2010 5:36 AM	Application	71 KB
original.img	11/3/2014 6:58 PM	IMG File	831,591 KB
ReadMe.txt	3/12/2014 4:29 PM	Text Document	8 KB
runner.bat	2/5/2013 8:53 PM	Windows Batch File	4 KB
zlib1.dll	5/13/2013 2:42 PM	Application extens...	105 KB

In above picture it is the structure of imagere packer tools

Name	Date modified	Type	Size
imgrepacker	3/12/2014 12:34 PM	File	90 KB
imgRePacker.exe	3/12/2014 4:36 PM	Application	120 KB
imgRePacker.ini	3/20/2015 4:34 PM	Configuration sett...	1 KB
lzma.exe	4/4/2010 5:36 AM	Application	71 KB
ReadMe.txt	3/12/2014 4:29 PM	Text Document	8 KB
runner.bat	2/5/2013 8:53 PM	Windows Batch File	4 KB
stockrom.img	11/3/2014 6:58 PM	IMG File	831,591 KB
zlib1.dll	5/13/2013 2:42 PM	Application extens...	105 KB

There are following steps to extract stock image.
1) change name of stock rom as original and run runner.bat

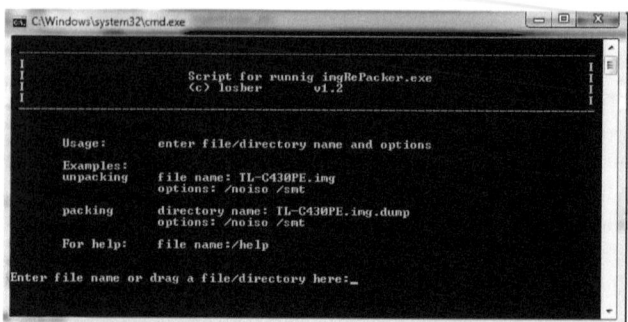

2) provide path of stock rom

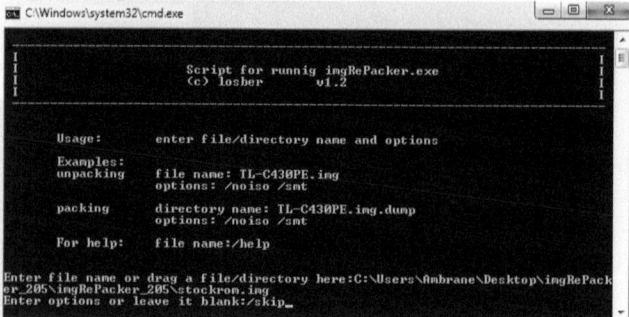

3) press enter
You can see it extracting all files in .fex format

```
"\boot0_sdcard.fex"              extracted (format: Allwinner BOOT0 file)
   "\u-boot.fex"             extracted (format: unknown)
   "\fes1.fex"               extracted (format: Allwinner BOOT0 file)
   "\usbtool.fex"            extracted (format: Windows PE file)
   "\aultools.fex"           extracted (format: Compiled lua file)
   "\aultls32.fex"           extracted (format: Compiled lua file)
   "\cardtool.fex"           extracted (format: Windows PE file)
   "\cardscript.fex"         extracted (format: unknown)
   "\sunxi_mbr.fex"          extracted (format: unknown)
   "\dlinfo.fex"             extracted (format: unknown)
   "\bootloader.fex"         extracted (format: FAT16 image)
         "bootloader.fex.iso"        created
   "\Wbootloader.fex"        extracted (format: unknown/empty?)
   "\env.fex"                extracted (format: unknown)
   "\Uenv.fex"               extracted (format: unknown/empty?)
   "\boot.fex"               extracted (format: Android boot image)
   "\Uboot.fex"              extracted (format: unknown/empty?)
   "\system.fex"             extracted (format: sparse image)
   "\Usystem.fex"            extracted (format: unknown/empty?)
   "\recovery.fex"           extracted (format: Android boot image)
   "\Urecovery.fex"          extracted (format: unknown/empty?)
   "\diskfs.fex"             extracted (format: unknown)
   "\data.fex"
```

This all .fex files are store in stockrom.img.dump folder

You can see in below picture

Name	Date modified	Type	Size
_iso	6/24/2015 4:07 PM	File folder	
aultls32.fex	6/24/2015 4:07 PM	FEX File	138 KB
aultools.fex	6/24/2015 4:07 PM	FEX File	151 KB
boot.fex	6/24/2015 4:07 PM	FEX File	8,768 KB
boot0_nand.fex	6/24/2015 4:07 PM	FEX File	32 KB
boot0_sdcard.fex	6/24/2015 4:07 PM	FEX File	32 KB
bootloader.fex	6/24/2015 4:07 PM	FEX File	4,477 KB
cardscript.fex	6/24/2015 4:07 PM	FEX File	2 KB
cardtool.fex	6/24/2015 4:07 PM	FEX File	80 KB
config.fex	6/24/2015 4:07 PM	FEX File	38 KB
data.fex	6/24/2015 4:07 PM	FEX File	288,865 KB
diskfs.fex	6/24/2015 4:07 PM	FEX File	1 KB
dlinfo.fex	6/24/2015 4:07 PM	FEX File	16 KB
env.fex	6/24/2015 4:07 PM	FEX File	128 KB
fes1.fex	6/24/2015 4:07 PM	FEX File	7 KB
image.cfg	6/24/2015 4:07 PM	CFG File	3 KB
recovery.fex	6/24/2015 4:07 PM	FEX File	11,692 KB
split_xxxx.fex	6/24/2015 4:07 PM	FEX File	1 KB
sunxi_mbr.fex	6/24/2015 4:07 PM	FEX File	64 KB
sys_config.fex	6/24/2015 4:07 PM	FEX File	59 KB
sys_partition.fex	6/24/2015 4:07 PM	FEX File	3 KB
system.fex	6/24/2015 4:07 PM	FEX File	516,136 KB
u-boot.fex	6/24/2015 4:07 PM	FEX File	736 KB
usbtool.fex	6/24/2015 4:07 PM	FEX File	130 KB

Here there four are four main files
1) **Boot.fex** – boot file contain all files which is necessary for boot like all boot script, boot logo, boot animation.

2) **Recovery.fex** – recovery file contain all back and restore files.
3) **System.fex** – folder all system files contain in system.
4) **Bootloader.fex** – this file contains script for boot, battery images and first boot logo file.

- **MTK Rom**

This rom is called mediateck rom and its get in many versionslike MT6577,MT6572,MT6575 and this is called MT65XX series. This rom is use currently in most of android devices.

- **Structure of MTK Rom**

Here this is the structure of MT6582 version.

Name	Date modified	Type	Size
APDB_MT6582_S01_KK1.MP1_	4/15/2015 11:31 AM	MP1_ File	159 KB
asd	4/15/2015 11:31 AM	Microsoft Office ...	24 KB
boot.img	4/15/2015 11:23 AM	IMG File	4,138 KB
BPLGUInfoCustomAppSrcP_MT6582_S00...	4/15/2015 11:30 AM	File	5,422 KB
cache.img	4/15/2015 11:31 AM	IMG File	6,169 KB
Checksum	7/1/2015 12:32 AM	Configuration sett...	0 KB
CheckSum_Gen	4/15/2015 11:31 AM	Application	136 KB
DbgInfo_WR8.W1315.MD.WG.MP_MBK82...	4/15/2015 11:31 AM	MP_MBK82_TB_JB...	982 KB
EBR1	7/1/2015 12:32 AM	File	0 KB
EBR2	7/1/2015 12:32 AM	File	0 KB
lk.bin	4/15/2015 11:31 AM	BIN File	238 KB
logo.bin	4/15/2015 11:31 AM	BIN File	382 KB
MBR	7/1/2015 12:32 AM	File	0 KB
MT6582_Android_scatter	4/15/2015 11:31 AM	Text Document	8 KB
preloader_mbk82_tb_kk.bin	4/15/2015 11:31 AM	BIN File	117 KB
recovery.img	4/15/2015 11:32 AM	IMG File	4,514 KB
secro.img	4/15/2015 11:31 AM	IMG File	132 KB
system.img	4/15/2015 2:42 PM	IMG File	894,854 KB
system.tmp	4/15/2015 1:32 PM	TMP File	331,671 KB
userdata.img	4/15/2015 2:43 PM	IMG File	17,885 KB

There are lots of files in MTK rom
1) **Boot.img-** boot file contain all files which is necessary for boot like all boot script, boot logo, boot animation.
2) **Recovery.img-** recovery file contain all back and restore files.
3) **System.img-** folder all system files contain in system.
4) **Logo.bin-** this file contains first boot logo.
5) **userdata.img-**The userdata.img file is a blank partition. It is used to reset the userdata partition to its factory state.ramdisk.img is a small partition image that is mounted

read-only by the kernel at boot time. It only contains /init and a few config files.

- **Structure and Extract Rockchip rom**

Rockchip also look like stock rom but structure is different and there are lots of versions of rockchip rom are available in market. We can see it file structure in below figure. It contains four main file like system, boot, recovery and kernel images.

Name	Date modified	Type	Size
boot.img	7/23/2015 11:10 AM	IMG File	1,015 KB
kernel.img	7/23/2015 11:10 AM	IMG File	7,549 KB
misc.img	7/23/2015 11:10 AM	IMG File	48 KB
recovery.img	7/23/2015 11:10 AM	IMG File	11,600 KB
system.img	7/23/2015 11:10 AM	IMG File	672,728 KB

1) **Boot.img** – boot file contain all files which is necessary for boot like all boot script, boot logo, boot animation.
2) **Recovery.img** – recovery file contain all back and restore files.
3) **System.img** – folder all system files contain in system.
4) **kernal.img** – this file contain all files related to android kernel.

There are following steps to extract rockchip rom.
1) extract factory tool and copy rockchip rom here.

Name	Date modified	Type	Size
FactoryToolV4.4	7/11/2015 8:22 AM	File folder	
FactoryToolV4.4	2/3/2015 1:38 PM	WinRAR archive	11,512 KB
new.img	2/3/2015 3:15 PM	IMG File	713,708 KB

2) run FWFactoryTool

Name	Date modified	Type	Size
bin	3/11/2014 3:15 PM	File folder	
config	3/11/2014 3:03 PM	File folder	
Doc	3/11/2014 3:03 PM	File folder	
Language	3/11/2014 3:03 PM	File folder	
Log	6/17/2014 1:23 AM	File folder	
Output	6/9/2014 12:40 AM	File folder	
Plugin	3/11/2014 3:04 PM	File folder	
config	6/9/2014 12:41 AM	Configuration sett...	1 KB
FWFactoryTool	3/11/2014 3:03 PM	Application	524 KB

3) Provide path of rockchip rom image file.

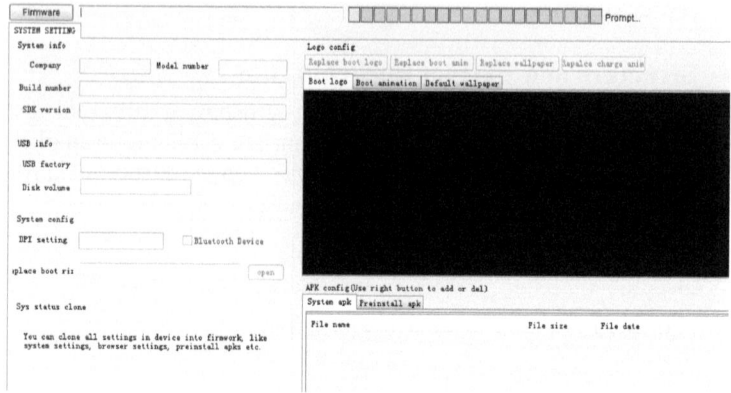

Here you can get out or extracted file in under the tool.

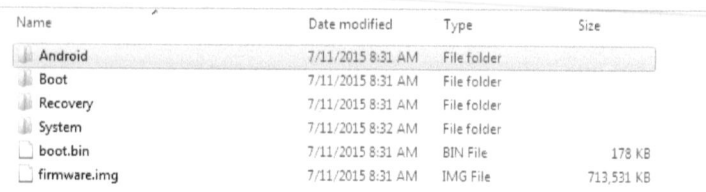

Unit 13: Structure and extract boot, bootloader, recovery and system file

- **Boot file**

Boot file contain ramdisk and kernel. This file is necessary to boot for any android device. The boot.img is part of the Android ROM you flash onto your device.

- **Structureof boot file**

It is a like a disk image. This is the part to enable boot to phone. Its include kernel and ram disk without this part phone it not able to boot.
We can see boot structure
There are 6 layer of Linux boot

```
BIOS
MBR
GRUB
Kernel
Init
Run level
```

BIOS
- BIOS include basic input-out system.
- It executes the bootloader program.
- Its look bootloader in floppy, cd rom and hard drive.
- Once boot loader program loaded in memory BIOS given full control to it.

MBR
- MBR stands for master boot Record.
- It is store in bootable disk.
- Its size less than 512.

GRUB
- GRUB stand for grand Unified Boot loader.
- If you install more than one kernel you can choose one of them.
- GRUB display splash screen.
- GRUB Configuration file located in **/boot/grub/grub.conf.**

Kernel
- Mounts the root file system.
- Kernel executes the /sbin/init program.

Init
- Its decide kernel run level.
- Run level

0-halt.
1-single user mode.
2-multiuser.
3-full multiuser mode.
4-unused.
5-X11
6-reboot
- -Identified the default initlevel and load all associate programs.

Runlevel Program
- it contains all runlevel programs.
- -Runlevel depend on default init level setting

Run level 0-/ete/rc.d/rc0.d/
Run level 1-/ete/rc.d/rc1.d/
Run level 2-/ete/rc.d/rc2.d/
Run level 3-/ete/rc.d/rc3.d/

Run level 4-/ete/rc.d/rc4.d/
Run level 5-/ete/rc.d/rc5.d/
Run level 6-/ete/rc.d/rc6.d/

- **Extract and repack boot file**

We can extract boot file by two type's first one by window command tools and other is by Linux command tools. There are lots of tools available to extract boot.img. For extract boot file firstly rename boot.fex to boot.img.

Extract and repack boot file by window command tools
We can extract boot.img bootimg tool.
Here there following steps to extract it.

1) extract bootimg.zip put bootimg.exe and boot.img file in test folder.

Name	Date modified	Type	Size
boot.img	1/4/2014 4:08 PM	IMG File	4,566 KB
bootimg.exe	4/20/2014 6:35 AM	Application	3,920 KB

2) now go in test folder and click Ctrl+Shift and right click and choose Open command window here.

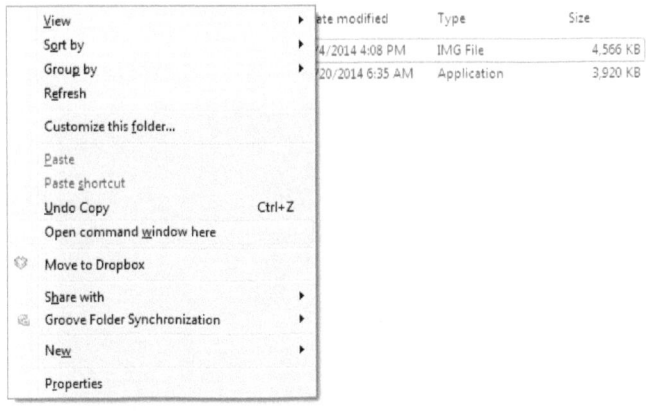

3) And write command **bootimg.exe –unpack-bootimg boot.img** and press enter

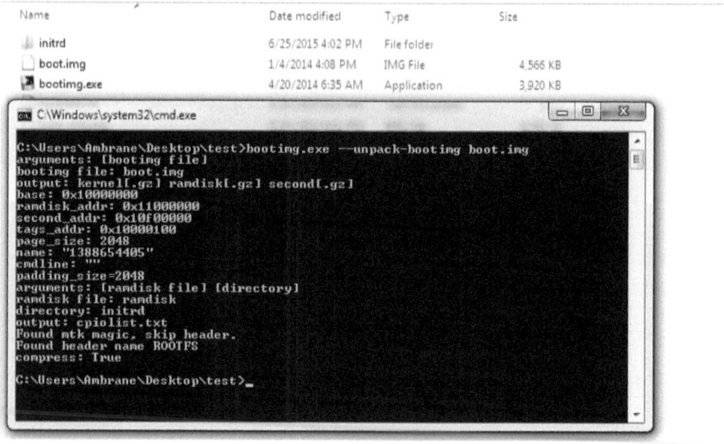

4) After edit file and folder in boot file we can Repack boot.img.

For repack boot file run this command **boot.img --repack-bootimg** And press enter.

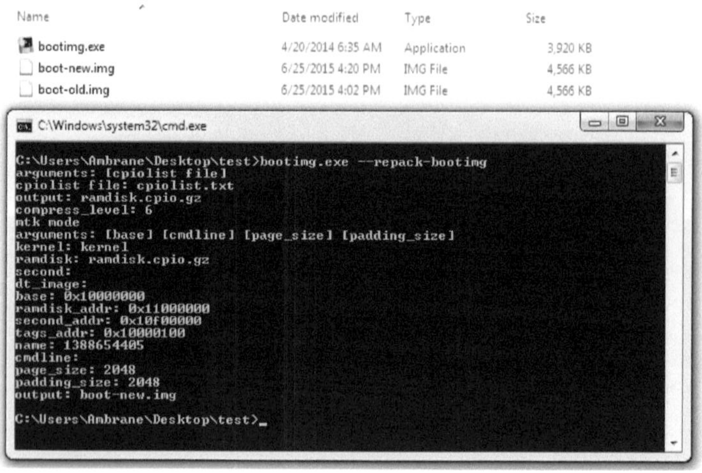

Here we get two files boot-new.img new boot file and boot-old.img old file.

Unit 13: Structure and extract boot, bootloader...

- **Recovery File**

Recovery file is a an android flash memory partition that use to perform factory reset or restore the original os and it provide clockwork mode to custom recovery for android Smart phone and tablet or we can say that its provide advanced recovery, installation, restoration and maintenance operation for device.

- **Recovery File Structure**

Recovery.img file contain many parts like install, Wipe, backup, restore and setting. Each part has own different role in android device. We will discuss later in on each part.

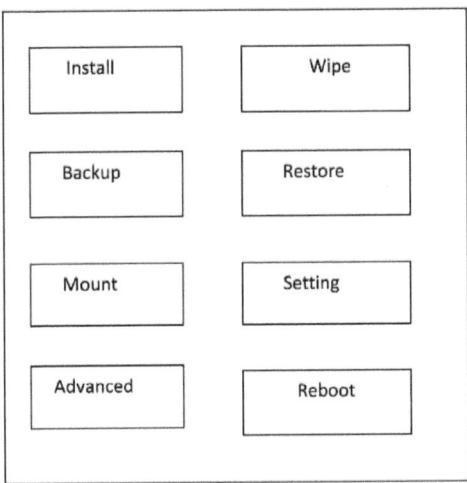

We can run recovery mode by adb command(adb recovery reboot) or with hard code button(by volume+ and power).

```
volume up/down to move highlight.
power button to select.

reboot system now
apply update from external storage
wipe data/factory reset
wipe cache partition
apply update from cache
recovery system from backup
update rkimage from /sdcard
```

There are the main functions of recovery file to manage android device.

Install - Install function contains to install any android device script to install any library or application.

```
Android system recovery <3e>

Choose a package to install:
/sdcard

../
Root_SuperSU.0.96.Only-signed.zip
Siyah-s2-v5.0.1-CWM.zip
.android_secure/
LOST.DIR/
```

Wipe - This function contain wide android data to device.
Backup - This function use to backup of android device.
Restore - This function use for restore any android device.
Mount - This function use to mount os files like sdcard files.
Setting -This function use to communicate device application.
Advanced - This function use for advance setting.
Reboot - This function use to reboot device.

- **Extract and repack Recovery File**

Here we will extract and repackrecovery file using Rk Firmware tools here there are some step to extract it.

1) extract rk firmware tool and copy recovery file here

Name	Date modified	Type	Size
bin	7/7/2015 12:52 PM	File folder	
Language	7/7/2015 12:52 PM	File folder	
root	7/7/2015 12:52 PM	File folder	
_bss	6/9/2013 11:43 PM	Windows Batch File	1 KB
DriverInstaller	9/12/2013 7:21 PM	Application	2,757 KB
freesize	6/9/2013 11:41 PM	Text Document	1 KB
recovery.img	12/2/2014 10:44 AM	IMG File	4,548 KB
sizes	8/11/2013 8:01 PM	Application	412 KB
src.src	9/13/2013 11:11 AM	SRC File	897 KB
START	9/13/2013 11:11 AM	Application	1,016 KB

Unit 13: Structure and extract boot, bootloader... | 131

2) run start file and press single tool

1) Select recovery file and press Extract then it will start automatically extract recovery file.

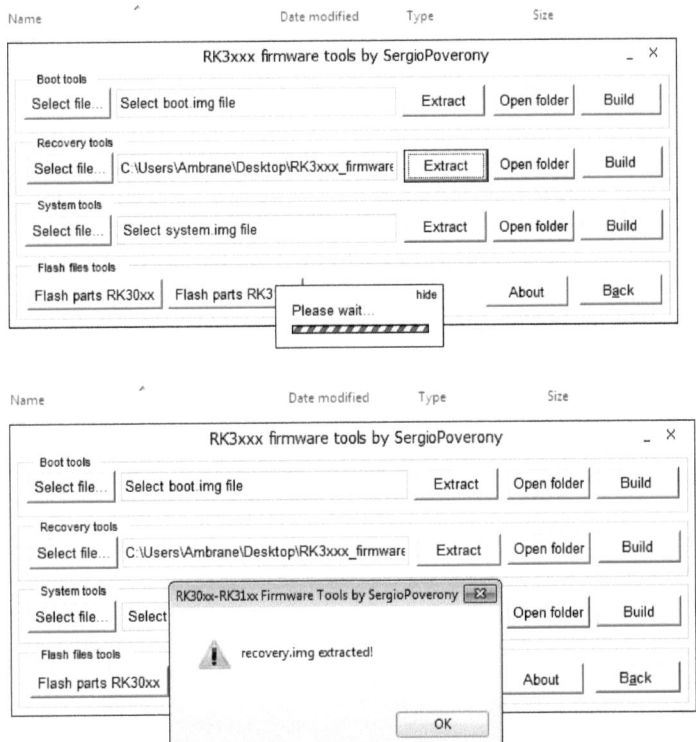

2) Here we can see extracted recovery file in temp folder

Name	Date modified	Type	Size
img-ramdisk	7/13/2015 4:01 PM	File folder	
recovery.img-cmdline	7/13/2015 4:01 PM	IMG-CMDLINE File	1 KB
zImage	7/13/2015 4:01 PM	File	7,480 KB

Name	Date modified	Type	Size
cloudsota	7/13/2015 4:01 PM	File folder	
data	7/13/2015 4:01 PM	File folder	
dev	7/13/2015 4:01 PM	File folder	
etc	7/13/2015 4:01 PM	File folder	
proc	7/13/2015 4:01 PM	File folder	
res	7/13/2015 4:01 PM	File folder	
sbin	7/13/2015 4:01 PM	File folder	
sys	7/13/2015 4:01 PM	File folder	
system	7/13/2015 4:01 PM	File folder	
tmp	7/13/2015 4:01 PM	File folder	
charger	7/13/2015 4:01 PM	File	271 KB
data	7/13/2015 4:01 PM	Text Document	1 KB
default.prop	7/13/2015 4:01 PM	PROP File	3 KB
disp.ko	7/13/2015 4:01 PM	KO File	5,386 KB
file_contexts	7/13/2015 4:01 PM	File	9 KB
fstab.sun8i	7/13/2015 4:01 PM	SUN8I File	3 KB
gslX680.ko	7/13/2015 4:01 PM	KO File	434 KB
gt818_ts.ko	7/13/2015 4:01 PM	KO File	333 KB
init	7/13/2015 4:01 PM	File	180 KB
init.rc	7/13/2015 4:01 PM	RC File	2 KB
init.recovery.sun8i.rc	7/13/2015 4:01 PM	RC File	1 KB
initlogo	7/13/2015 4:01 PM	RLE File	1,500 KB
lcd.ko	7/13/2015 4:01 PM	KO File	442 KB
nand.ko	7/13/2015 4:01 PM	KO File	1,480 KB

3) After edit we can also repack recovery file using press build button. we can see it in root directory.

Name	Date modified	Type	Size
bin	7/7/2015 12:52 PM	File folder	
Language	7/7/2015 12:52 PM	File folder	
root	7/7/2015 12:52 PM	File folder	
temp	7/13/2015 5:06 PM	File folder	
_bss	6/9/2013 11:43 PM	Windows Batch File	1 KB
DriverInstaller	9/12/2013 7:21 PM	Application	2,757 KB
freesize	6/9/2013 11:41 PM	Text Document	1 KB
new_recovery.img	7/13/2015 5:07 PM	IMG File	11,760 KB
recovery.img	5/16/2015 3:17 PM	IMG File	11,738 KB
sizes	8/11/2013 8:01 PM	Application	412 KB
src.src	9/13/2013 11:11 AM	SRC File	897 KB
START	9/13/2013 11:11 AM	Application	1,016 KB

Unit 13: Structure and extract boot, bootloader... | 133

- **System file**

this file contains the entire Android OS, other than the kernel and the ramdisk. This includes the Android

GUI and all the system applications that come pre-installed on the device.

```
Administrator: C:\Windows\system32\cmd.exe - adb shell

D:\adt-bundle-windows-x86-20130717\sdk\platform-tools>adb devices
List of devices attached
0123456789ABCDEF        device

D:\adt-bundle-windows-x86-20130717\sdk\platform-tools>adb shell
shell@android:/ $ cd /system
cd /system
shell@android:/system $ ls
ls
app
bin
build.prop
data
etc
fonts
framework
lib
lost+found
media
mobile_toolkit
res
tts
usr
```

- **Extract and repacksystem file**

Here we will extract and repack system file using Rk Firmware tools here there are some step to extract it.

1) extract rk firmware tool and copy system file here

Name	Date modified	Type	Size
bin	7/7/2015 12:52 PM	File folder	
Language	7/7/2015 12:52 PM	File folder	
root	7/7/2015 12:52 PM	File folder	
temp	7/13/2015 4:01 PM	File folder	
_bss	6/9/2013 11:43 PM	Windows Batch File	1 KB
DriverInstaller	9/12/2013 7:21 PM	Application	2,757 KB
freesize	6/9/2013 11:41 PM	Text Document	1 KB
sizes	8/11/2013 8:01 PM	Application	412 KB
src.src	9/13/2013 11:11 AM	SRC File	897 KB
START	9/13/2013 11:11 AM	Application	1,016 KB
system.img	12/31/2014 4:26 AM	IMG File	822,995 KB

2) run start file and press single tool

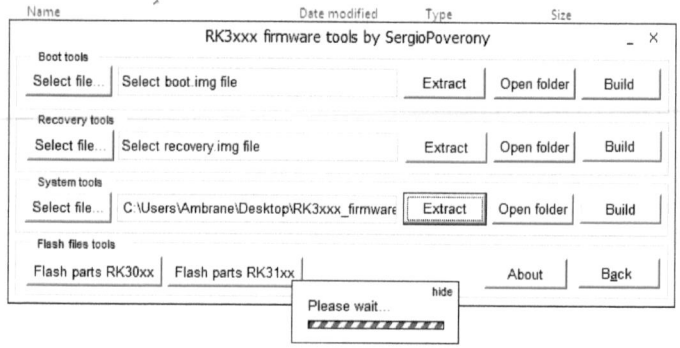

3) Select system file and press Extract then it will start automatically extract system file.

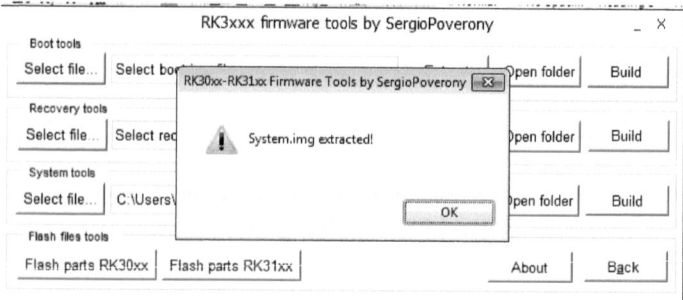

4) Here we can see extracted system file in temp folder

Unit 13: Structure and extract boot, bootloader... | 135

Name	Date modified	Type	Size
system	7/13/2015 4:57 PM	File folder	

Name	Date modified	Type	Size
app	7/13/2015 4:54 PM	File folder	
appbackup	7/13/2015 4:54 PM	File folder	
bin	7/13/2015 4:54 PM	File folder	
data	7/13/2015 4:54 PM	File folder	
etc	7/13/2015 4:54 PM	File folder	
extra	7/13/2015 4:54 PM	File folder	
fonts	7/13/2015 4:54 PM	File folder	
framework	7/13/2015 4:55 PM	File folder	
lib	7/13/2015 4:54 PM	File folder	
lost+found	7/13/2015 4:54 PM	File folder	
media	7/13/2015 4:54 PM	File folder	
mobile_toolkit	7/13/2015 4:54 PM	File folder	
priv-app	7/13/2015 4:55 PM	File folder	
res	7/13/2015 4:54 PM	File folder	
tts	7/13/2015 4:54 PM	File folder	
usr	7/13/2015 4:54 PM	File folder	
vendor	7/13/2015 4:54 PM	File folder	
xbin	7/13/2015 4:54 PM	File folder	
build.prop	7/13/2015 4:54 PM	PROP File	4 KB

Type: PROP File

5) After edit we can also repack system file using press build button. we can see it in root directory.

Name	Date modified	Type	Size
bin	7/7/2015 12:52 PM	File folder	
Language	7/7/2015 12:52 PM	File folder	
root	7/7/2015 12:52 PM	File folder	
temp	7/13/2015 4:57 PM	File folder	
_bss	6/9/2013 11:43 PM	Windows Batch File	1 KB
DriverInstaller	9/12/2013 7:21 PM	Application	2,757 KB
freesize	6/9/2013 11:41 PM	Text Document	1 KB
new_system.img	7/13/2015 5:02 PM	IMG File	822,995 KB
sizes	8/11/2013 8:01 PM	Application	412 KB
src.src	9/13/2013 11:11 AM	SRC File	897 KB
START	9/13/2013 11:11 AM	Application	1,016 KB
system.img	12/31/2014 4:26 AM	IMG File	822,995 KB

- **Bootloader file**

A bootloader is a computer program that loads an operating system (OS) or runtime environment for the android device.

bootloader is code that is executed before any Operating System starts to run. Bootloaders basically package the instructions to boot operating system kernel and most of them also have their own debugging and modification environment.

- **Structure of Bootloader file**

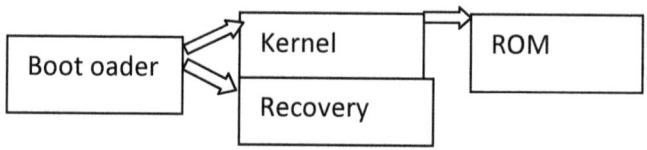

- **Extract and repack bootloader file**

Here there are some step to extract and repack bootloader file.

1) Firstly install powerIso software and copy bootloader.img file in separate folder.

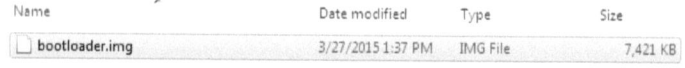

2) Right click and select PowerIso and then select extract here.

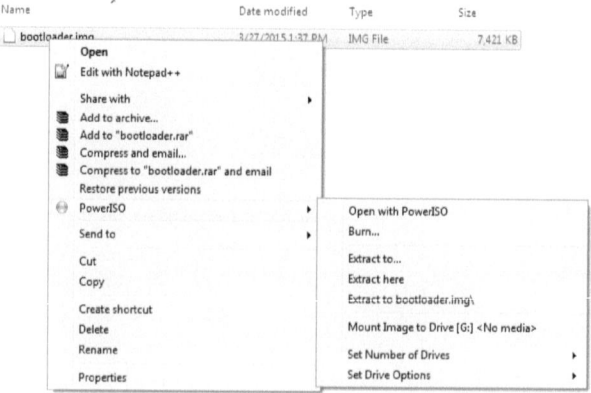

3) Here you can see expected bootloder file.

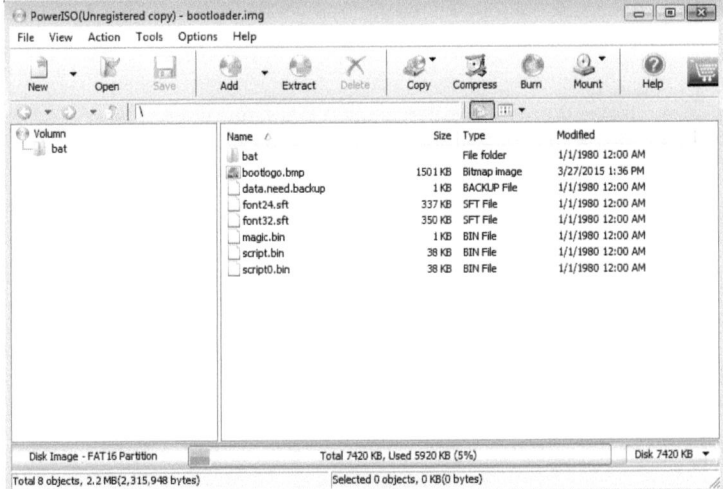

Here you can save extracted file and also we can directly bootloader file.

- **Extract and repack boot file in ubuntu**

Here there are some step to extract boot file in ububtu system.

1) Copy boot, recovery and system file in folder custom rom.

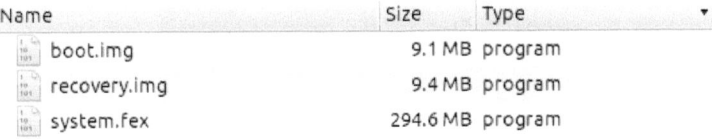

2) Copy tools in this folder here.

138 | Android Firmware Customization

3) Extract tools.zip file here.

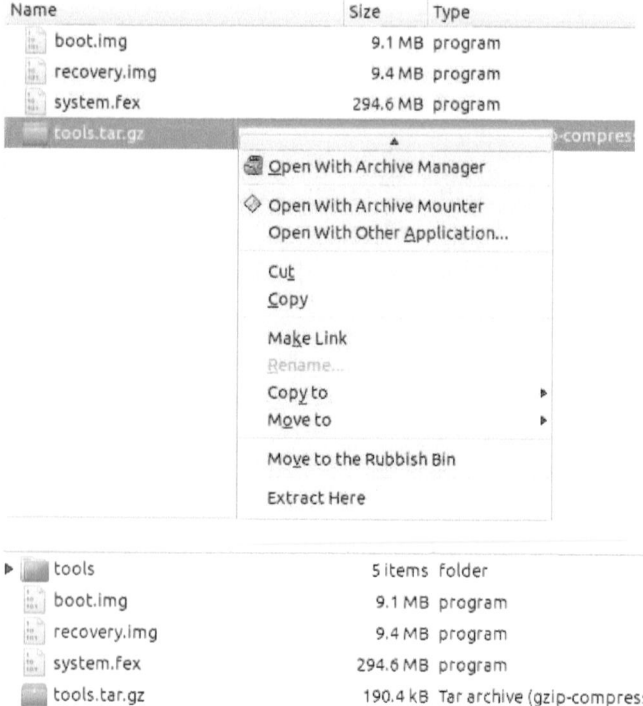

4) Open terminal application.

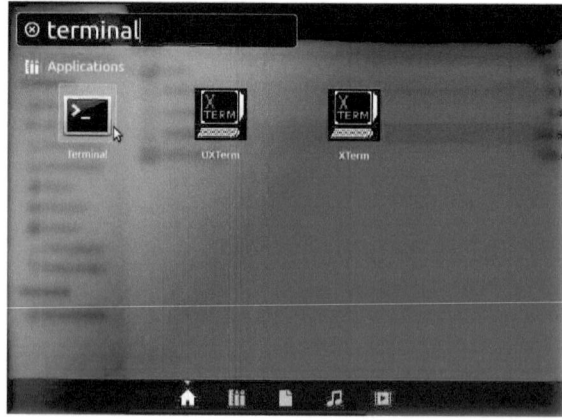

Unit 13: Structure and extract boot, bootloader... | 139

5) For extract boot file go to custom folder using command
   $ cd "custom rom"
   And extract boot file using command
   $ tools/split_bootimg.pl boot.img
   And type command ls to check files in directory
   $ ls
   Here you can see ramdisk.zip file here.

```
miniand@miniand:~$ cd "custom image"
miniand@miniand:~/custom image$ tools/split_bootimg.pl boot.img
Page size: 2048 (0x00000800)
Kernel size: 8094708 (0x007b83f4)
Ramdisk size: 979799 (0x000ef357)
Second size: 0 (0x00000000)
Board name:
Command line: console=ttyS0,115200 rw init=/init loglevel=8
Writing boot.img-kernel ... complete.
Writing boot.img-ramdisk.gz ... complete.
miniand@miniand:~/custom image$ ls
boot.img          boot.img-ramdisk.gz  system.fex   tools.tar.gz
boot.img-kernel   recovery.img         tools
miniand@miniand:~/custom image$
```

6) Now we will extract ramdisk file using these command
   Firstly we will create a directory using command
   $ mkdir ramdisk
   Go to ramdisk folder using command
   $ cd ramdisk
   Now we will extract ramdisk.zip file using command
   $ gunzip –c ../boot.img-ramdisk.gz | cpio –i
   And check ramdisk files using ls command
   $ ls

```
miniand@miniand:~/custom image$ mkdir ramdisk
miniand@miniand:~/custom image$ cd ramdisk
miniand@miniand:~/custom image/ramdisk$ gunzip -c ../boot.img-ramdisk.gz | c
pio -i
7739 blocks
miniand@miniand:~/custom image/ramdisk$ ls
data          init.goldfish.rc  init.sun4i.usb.rc  system
default.prop  initlogo.rle      proc               ueventd.goldfish.rc
dev           init.rc           sbin               ueventd.rc
init          init.sun4i.rc     sys                ueventd.sun4i.rc
miniand@miniand:~/custom image/ramdisk$
```

Now are able to edit as need

7) Now we can rebuild boot file using following command
   $ cd ..
   $ tools/mkbootfs ramdisk | gzip > ramdisk-new.gz
   $ tools/mkbootimg --base 0x40000000 --kernel boot.img-kernel --ramdisk ramdisk-new.gz --cmdline 'console=ttyS0,115200 tw init=/init loglevel=8' -o new-boot.img
   $ ls

```
miniand@miniand:~/custom image$ tools/mkbootfs ramdisk | gzip > ramdisk-new.gz
miniand@miniand:~/custom image$ tools/mkbootimg --base 0x40000000 --kernel boot.img-kernel --ramdisk ramdisk-new.gz --cmdline 'console=ttyS0,115200 rw init=/init loglevel=8' -o new-boot.img
miniand@miniand:~/custom image$ ls
boot.img              new-boot.img      recovery.img   tools.tar.gz
boot.img-kernel       ramdisk           system.fex
boot.img-ramdisk.gz   ramdisk-new.gz    tools
miniand@miniand:~/custom image$
```

- **Extract and repack recovery file in ubuntu**
1) Here we can also extract recovery file using following command
   $ tools/split_bootimg.pl recovery.img
   $ rm -rf ramdisk
   $ mkdir ramdisk
   $ cd ramdisk
   $ gunzip -c ../recovery.img-ramdisk.gz | cpio -i
   $ ls

```
miniand@miniand:~/custom image$ tools/split_bootimg.pl recovery.img
Page size: 2048 (0x00000800)
Kernel size: 8094708 (0x007b83f4)
Ramdisk size: 1310269 (0x0013fe3d)
Second size: 0 (0x00000000)
Board name:
Command line: console=ttyS0,115200 rw init=/init loglevel=8
Writing recovery.img-kernel ... complete.
Writing recovery.img-ramdisk.gz ... complete.
miniand@miniand:~/custom image$ rm -rf ramdisk
miniand@miniand:~/custom image$ mkdir ramdisk
miniand@miniand:~/custom image$ cd ramdisk
miniand@miniand:~/custom image/ramdisk$ gunzip -c ../recovery.img-ramdisk.gz | cpio -i
8607 blocks
miniand@miniand:~/custom image/ramdisk$ ls
data            init           res       tmp
default.prop    initlogo.rle   sbin      ueventd.goldfish.rc
dev             init.rc        sys       ueventd.rc
etc             proc           system    ueventd.sun4i.rc
miniand@miniand:~/custom image/ramdisk$
```

2) After done all modification we can also rebuild recovery file again
    $ cd ..
    $ tools/mkbootfs ramdisk | gzip > ramdisk-new.gz
    $ tools/mkbootimg --base 0x40000000 --kernel recovery.img-kernel --ramdisk ramdisk-new.gz --cmdline 'console=ttyS0, 115200 rw init=/init loglevel=8' -o new-recovery.img
    $ ls

```
miniand@miniand:~/custom image/ramdisk$ cd ..
miniand@miniand:~/custom image$ tools/mkbootfs ramdisk | gzip > ramdisk-new.gz
miniand@miniand:~/custom image$ tools/mkbootimg  --base 0x40000000 --kernel recovery.img-kernel --ramdisk ramdisk-new.gz --cmdline 'console=ttyS0,115200 rw init=/init loglevel=8' -o new-recovery.img
miniand@miniand:~/custom image$ ls
boot.img              ramdisk                  system.fex
boot.img-kernel       ramdisk-new.gz           tools
boot.img-ramdisk.gz   recovery.img             tools.tar.gz
new-boot.img          recovery.img-kernel
new-recovery.img      recovery.img-ramdisk.gz
miniand@miniand:~/custom image$
```

- **Extract and repack system file in ubuntu**

1) We can extract also system file using following command
    $ tools/simg2img system.fex system.img
    $ mkdir system
    $ sudo mount -o loop system.img system
    $ cd system
    $ ls
    And output of program is below

```
miniand@miniand:~/custom image$ tools/simg2img system.fex system.img
computed crc32 of 0xc37c0664, expected 0x00000000
miniand@miniand:~/custom image$ mkdir system
miniand@miniand:~/custom image$ sudo mount -o loop system.img system
[sudo] password for miniand:
miniand@miniand:~/custom image$ cd system
miniand@miniand:~/custom image/system$ ls
app  build.prop  fonts       lib     preinstall  usr      xbin
bin  etc         framework   media   tts         vendor
miniand@miniand:~/custom image/system$
```

2) After done all modification we can repack again system file using following commands
    $ cd ../tools
    $ sudo ./mkuserimg.sh -s ../system ../new-system.fex ext4 ../tmp 300M

```
$ cd ..
$ sudo umount system
$ ls
```

Here 300 is the size of system file. It may more than 300 if size of system file is large. Its depend on version of android device its around 500 for jellybean devices.

```
miniand@miniand:~/custom image/tools$ sudo ./mkuserimg.sh -s ../system ../n
ew-system.fex ext4 ../tmp 300M
in mkuserimg.sh PATH=/usr/local/sbin:/usr/local/bin:/usr/sbin:/usr/bin:/sbi
n:/bin
./make_ext4fs -s -l 300M -a ../tmp ../new-system.fex ../system
Creating filesystem with parameters:
    Size: 314572800
    Block size: 4096
    Blocks per group: 32768
    Inodes per group: 6400
    Inode size: 256
    Journal blocks: 1200
    Label:
    Blocks: 76800
    Block groups: 3
    Reserved block group size: 23
Created filesystem with 1281/19200 inodes and 71780/76800 blocks
miniand@miniand:~/custom image/tools$ cd ..
miniand@miniand:~/custom image$ ls
boot.img              ramdisk                  system.fex
boot.img-kernel       ramdisk-new.gz           system.img
boot.img-ramdisk.gz   recovery.img             tools
new-boot.img          recovery.img-kernel      tools.tar.gz
new-recovery.img      recovery.img-ramdisk.gz
new-system.fex        system
miniand@miniand:~/custom image$
```

Unit 14: Android Rooting

- **What is android rooting**

Android rooting is a process which break manufacture device limitation or in other work it is like a jell break. After rooting process user can edit, delete or update system files or directory. This process provide super user permission to user. It is same like sudo command in Linux and root word come from Unix/Linux.

- **Root Advantages**

There are following advantage of android rooting.

1) **Custom Rom/Firmware**
   Rom is a software which run on your device so after root we can do anything in rom just like we can edit, delete or update rom files and we can also flash rom. We can also change device boot process like boot logo and boot animation.

2) **Custom Theme**
   We can also change android launcher or we can change Device theme.

3) **Kernel, Speed and Battery**
   After root we can flash device kernel and we also improve speed of device or battery performance.

4) **Backup/Restore**
   We can also back device data and applications of our device.

5) **Unlocked other Feature**
   We can unlock other feature like we can add or delete system application or some application which require root permission may be perfectly run in rooted device.

- **Root Disadvantages**

There are following Disadvantages of rooting

4) Break Device Warranty

After root you may be lost your device warranty because many manufacture or developer does not allow device rooting.

5) Security

After rooting process you lost your security because it may be unwanted person can change your device files any one can modify your rom.

- **How Check Device root or not**

The main question is that how we can check a device root or not. We can check it by type's first one is that there are lot of application available in android market for check root and other by android command.

Ex: adb shell

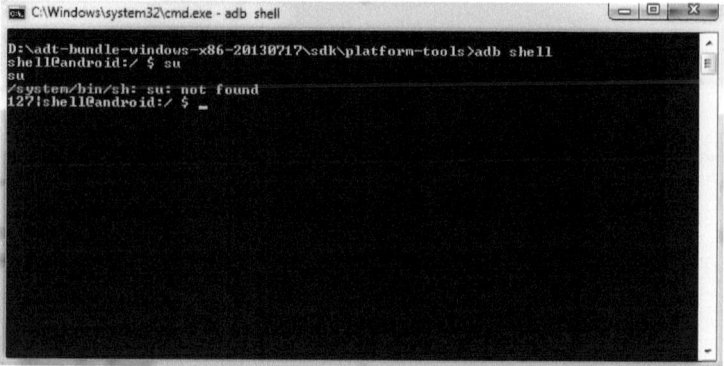

For the above picture we can see that when we run adb shell command we find here two symbol first one is # and second one is $. # indicate that device is already rooted and $ indicate device in unroot.

- **How To Root**

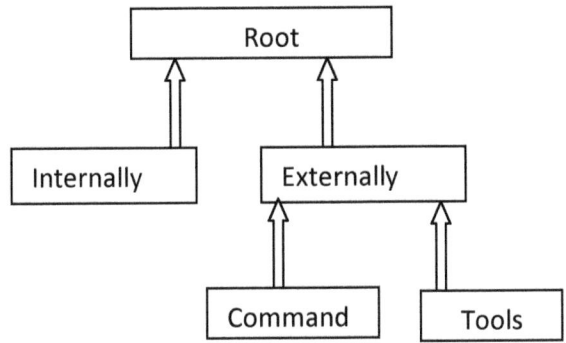

From the above picture it clear that We can root a device in types by internally or Externally.

Internally Means if we have device original firmware we can root or Device rom we can root whole operating system by changing some files and in externally root we can root device by applying some command or by some tools. In externally root it may be root or no because you already know that in currently market. There are lot of android rom available in market like stock rom, rockchip rom, MTK rom and each rom has different structure or file format or it may be it require some additional user permission so that why it may be root or not by commands or tools.

- **Internally or rom root**

If have already discuss that if have original device rom so can root it. For root externally we have to extract rom and we will need default.prop file. Generally we can find it in boot.img or recovery.in.

You can better understand with below pictures.

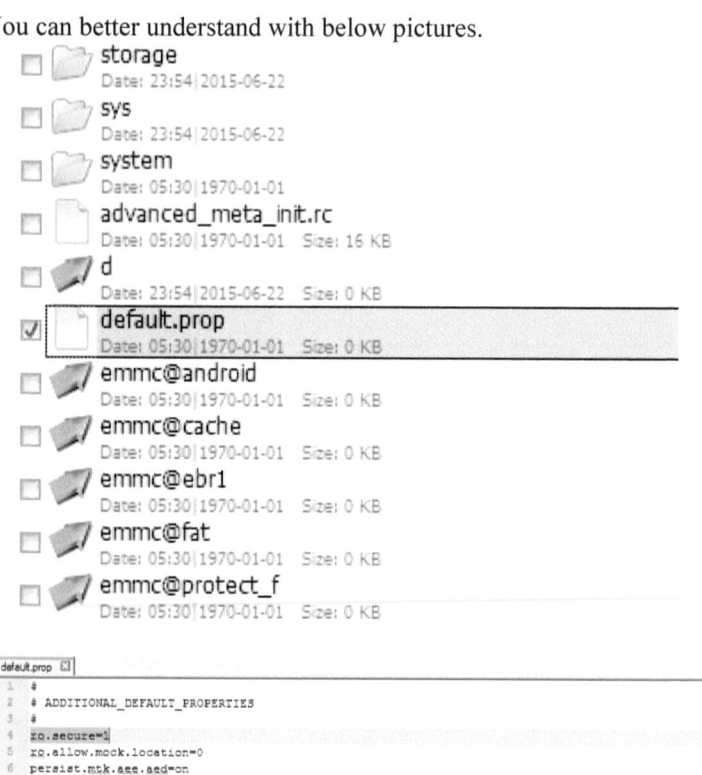

In last picture you can see that there is line **ro.secure=1**. If this is 1 means that its secure or unroot but if its value is 0 it means is unsecure or root. So we will have to change this value for root.
We can change this value by adb command

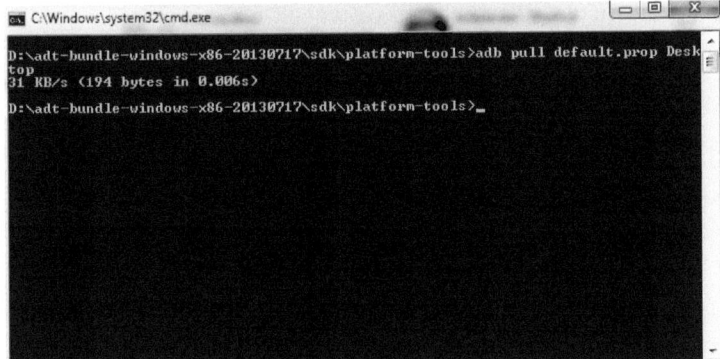

From this pull command we copy default.prop file in to desktop. Now we can edit this value and again insert in to device by push command.

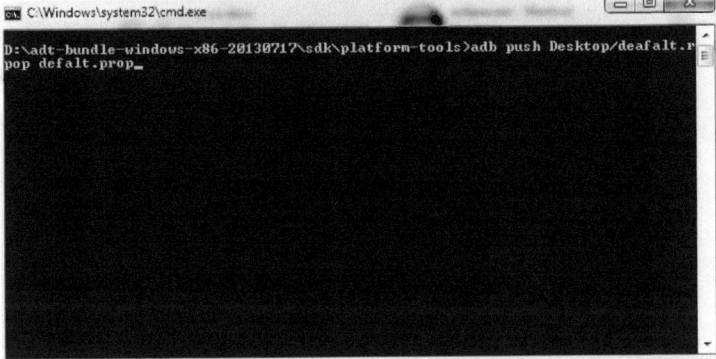

- **Externally Root**

We can also externally root a device by two types by tools or adb command. There are lot of rooting tools available in market at this time like kingo root, one click super user tools but we are sure about rooting tools because we already know that each rom has different directory structure.

Other for root by adb command we will have need three files
1) su
2) busybox
3) superuser.apk

Now copy busybox, su and superuser.apk to **/data/local/tmp/** using adb command

You can see it in below picture

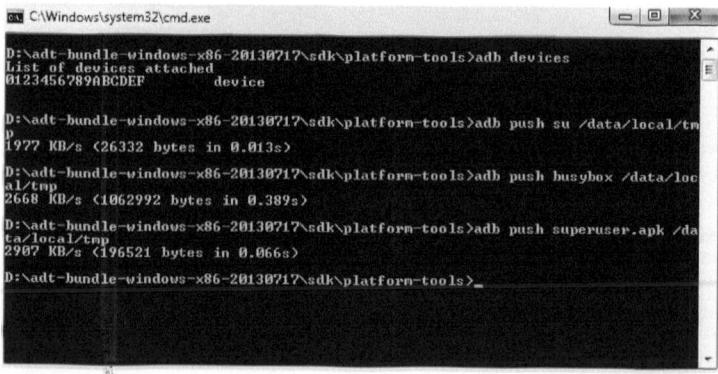

Now run adb shell command it still show $ sign means it is unroot still.
Now run other command like
Chmod 6755 /data/local/tmp/su
Chmod 755 /data/local/tmp/bustbox
Chmod 644 /data/local/tmp/superuser.apk

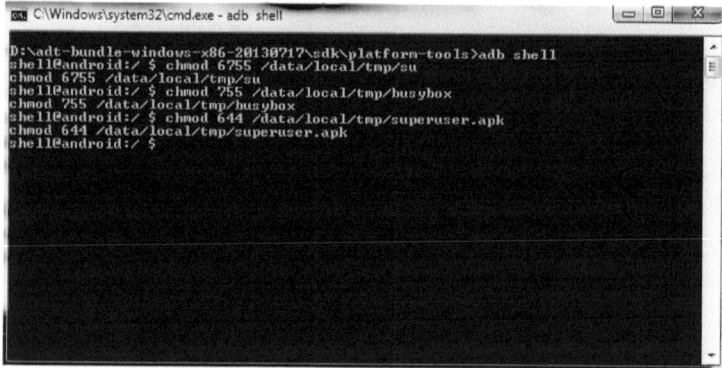

For further you will have to need Linux distro with nautilus(Linux ubuntu 11.04)

Now turn reboot your device.

Now connect your device with ubuntu.

Run command

Sudo nautiluson obuntu terminal

Now put your device in to recovery mode by press power and volume + button simultaneously.

Run both command on ubuntu terminal.

Move/cut-paste su and busybox to /system/bin/ using Nautilus.

Move/cut-paste Superuser.apk to /system/app/ using Nautilus.

Turn off your device and again connect with window device and run **adb shell su** command now your device must be rooted.

You can see it in below picture.

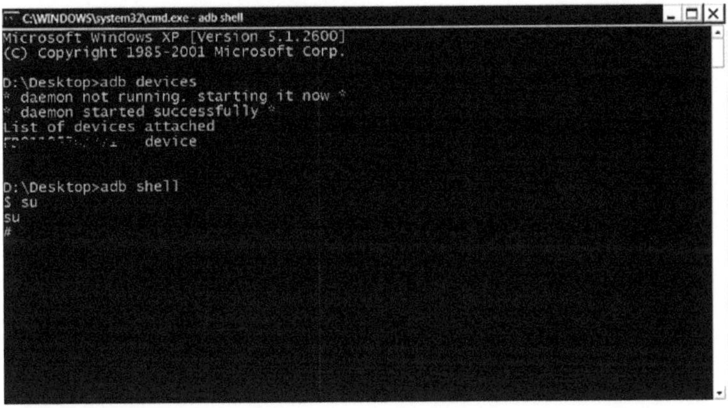

```
C:\WINDOWS\system32\cmd.exe - adb shell
Microsoft Windows XP [Version 5.1.2600]
(C) Copyright 1985-2001 Microsoft Corp.

D:\Desktop>adb devices
* daemon not running. starting it now *
* daemon started successfully *
List of devices attached
                        device

D:\Desktop>adb shell
$ su
su
#
```

Unit 15 : Boot animation

- **Boot animation**

The boot animation is the first screen that you see when power on your Android phone or tablet. It may be a zip file or video file. Its show manufacture logo on boot screen and its run after the boot logo.

The Android boot animation is contained an uncompressed zip file as bootanimation.zip that can be found in the media folder of the system /system/media on the device.

This single file contains all the information about to run the boot animationand is loaded automatically when the device boots.

you can see boot animation directory in below picture.

Name	Date modified	Type	Size
app	7/14/2015 4:33 PM	File folder	
bin	7/14/2015 4:35 PM	File folder	
data	7/14/2015 4:35 PM	File folder	
etc	7/14/2015 4:35 PM	File folder	
fonts	7/14/2015 4:35 PM	File folder	
framework	7/14/2015 4:35 PM	File folder	
install	7/14/2015 4:34 PM	File folder	
lib	7/14/2015 4:34 PM	File folder	
lost+found	7/14/2015 4:35 PM	File folder	
media	7/14/2015 4:35 PM	File folder	
mobile_toolkit	7/14/2015 4:34 PM	File folder	
prebuilt	7/14/2015 4:34 PM	File folder	
priv-app	7/14/2015 4:34 PM	File folder	
res	7/14/2015 4:35 PM	File folder	
tts	7/14/2015 4:35 PM	File folder	
usr	7/14/2015 4:35 PM	File folder	
vendor	7/14/2015 4:35 PM	File folder	
xbin	7/14/2015 4:35 PM	File folder	
build.prop	7/14/2015 4:35 PM	PROP File	4 KB

Name	Date modified	Type	Size
audio	7/14/2015 4:35 PM	File folder	
bootanimation	7/14/2015 5:34 PM	File folder	
images	7/14/2015 4:35 PM	File folder	
video	7/14/2015 4:35 PM	File folder	
bootanimation.zip	7/14/2015 4:35 PM	zip Archive	799 KB
bootaudio.mp3	7/14/2015 4:35 PM	MP3 Format Sound	54 KB

Unit 15: Boot animation | 151

- **Structure of Boot animation**

If you extract the contents of the bootanimation.zip file to your computer, you will see

1) Desc.txt file
2) Part 0 folder(contain png or jpeg images in order form)
3) More part 1, part 2 folder(it may be present or not)

The animation is played simply by displaying the images in a sequence, and the text file defines how they are to be show images in device screen.

Folder

These contain PNG or Jpeg images in order, starting from like 0000.jpg or 00001.jpg and proceeding with increments one by one.

There should minimum at least one folder in bootanimation.zip you can see all contain in folder in below picture

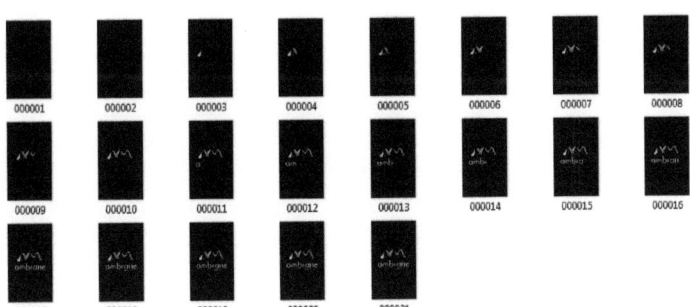

Desc.txt file

This file defines how the images in the folder are display in during the boot time.

You can see format of desc.txt file format in below picture.

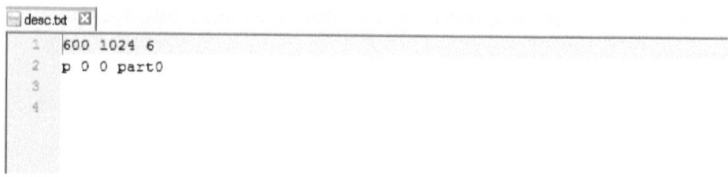

As you can see, in the first line, 600 and 1024 define the width and height of the boot animation in pixels and

It is depend on device screen resolution 6 is the frame rate in fps (frames per second) number of images to display per second.

The second and line p represent part of animation and end with part0 or part1 and 0 represent how many times this part will loop before switching to the next part (if exist) and here 0 number represent it will run infinite till boot complete and 1 represent it will run single time and hang in last image till boot. Send number 0 is for pause and it represent in frame.

A pause of 5 for example, would mean pausing for the time it takes 5 frames to play and since the frame rate is 6 frames per second.

We can better understand with below picture.

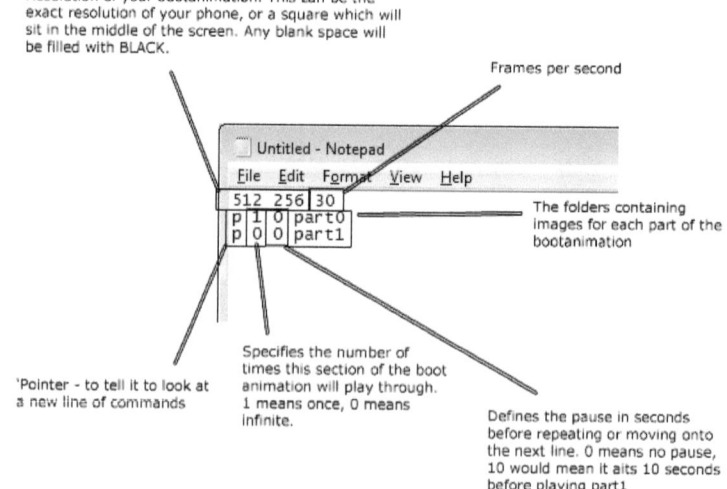

• Create boot animation

We can easily create device boot animation in zip file format.

Here there are some steps to create boot animation.zip file

1) For create boot animation for device firstly we will have to install WinZip software in pc.

2) Copy all image in a folder as name part 0 in order format then create desc.txt and write according device configuration and user requirement as previous topic structure of boot animation.

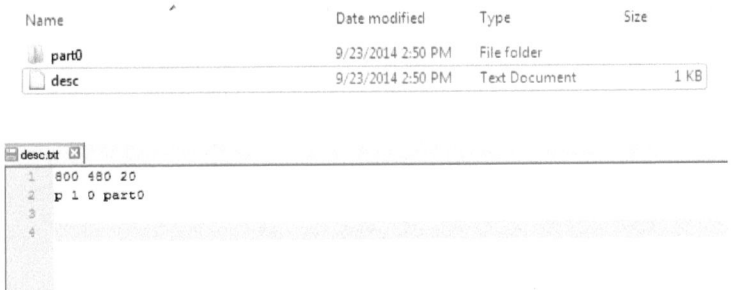

3) Then select part0 folder and desc.txt file and right click here according below picture.

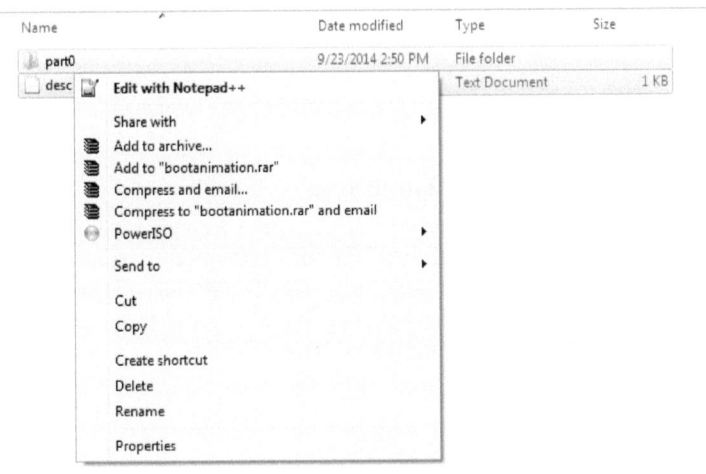

4) Then choose add to archive and check zip & select store in compression method then ok

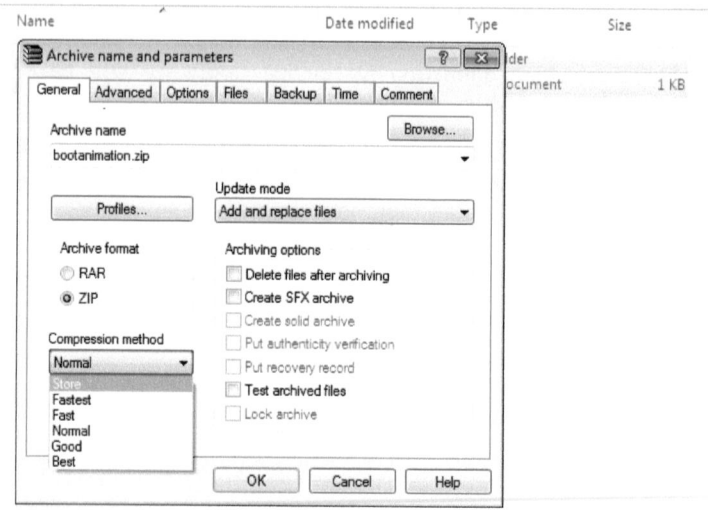

5) Here we will get a uncompressed zip file.

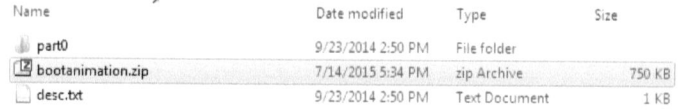

- **Change boot animation in rom**

If you have original rom of your device then we can easily replace custom boot animation with original boot animation of your device. For this process Extract system.img file of android rom and open system folder and then select media folder you put this zip file in this directory then again compress system.img file .

Name	Date modified	Type	Size
audio	7/14/2015 4:35 PM	File folder	
bootanimation	7/14/2015 5:34 PM	File folder	
images	7/14/2015 4:35 PM	File folder	
video	7/14/2015 4:35 PM	File folder	
bootanimation.zip	7/14/2015 4:35 PM	zip Archive	799 KB
bootaudio.mp3	7/14/2015 4:35 PM	MP3 Format Sound	54 KB

- **Change boot animation with adb command**

We can also replace you custom boot animation with adb command if your device is rooted.

Open command promote of pc and adb push <path of bootanimation.zip> system/media/bootanimation.zip

```
D:\adt-bundle-windows-x86-20130717\sdk\platform-tools>adb devices
List of devices attached
0123456789ABCDEF        device

D:\adt-bundle-windows-x86-20130717\sdk\platform-tools>adb push bootanimation.zip
 sytem/media/bootanimation.zip_
```

Unit 16 : Boot logo

- **Boot logo**

The boot animation is the first screen that you see when power on your Android phone or tablet. It may be a .bmp file or .rle file. Its show manufacture logo on boot screen and its run after the boot logo.

It may be different structure in different rom and it may one or two boot logo exist in rom.

- **Boot logo in stock rom**

There may be exist two boot logo in android stock rom.

First boot logo

First boot log in stock rom exist in bootloader file in form .bmp format.

Name	Size	Type	Modified
bat		File folder	1/1/1980 12:00 AM
bootlogo.bmp	1501 KB	Bitmap image	3/27/2015 1:36 PM
data.need.backup	1 KB	BACKUP File	1/1/1980 12:00 AM
font24.sft	337 KB	SFT File	1/1/1980 12:00 AM
font32.sft	350 KB	SFT File	1/1/1980 12:00 AM
magic.bin	1 KB	BIN File	1/1/1980 12:00 AM
script.bin	38 KB	BIN File	1/1/1980 12:00 AM
script0.bin	38 KB	BIN File	1/1/1980 12:00 AM

Second boot logo

second boot logo in stock exist in boot file in form of .rle format.

res	7/15/2015 3:17 PM	File folder	
sbin	7/15/2015 3:17 PM	File folder	
sys	7/15/2015 3:17 PM	File folder	
system	7/15/2015 3:17 PM	File folder	
charger	7/15/2015 3:17 PM	File	271 KB
default.prop	7/15/2015 3:17 PM	PROP File	1 KB
file_contexts	7/15/2015 3:17 PM	File	9 KB
fstab.sun8i	7/15/2015 3:17 PM	SUN8I File	3 KB
init	7/15/2015 3:17 PM	File	180 KB
init.environ.rc	7/15/2015 3:17 PM	RC File	1 KB
init.rc	7/15/2015 3:17 PM	RC File	23 KB
init.recovery.sun8i.rc	7/15/2015 3:17 PM	RC File	1 KB
init.sun8i.rc	7/15/2015 3:17 PM	RC File	8 KB
init.sun8i.usb.rc	7/15/2015 3:17 PM	RC File	4 KB
init.sunxi.3gdongle.rc	7/15/2015 3:17 PM	RC File	1 KB
init.trace.rc	7/15/2015 3:17 PM	RC File	2 KB
init.usb.rc	7/15/2015 3:17 PM	RC File	4 KB
initlogo.rle	7/15/2015 3:17 PM	RLE File	1,500 KB
nand.ko	7/15/2015 3:17 PM	KO File	1,480 KB
property_contexts	7/15/2015 3:17 PM	File	3 KB
seapp_contexts	7/15/2015 3:17 PM	File	1 KB
sepolicy	7/15/2015 3:17 PM	File	74 KB
ueventd.rc	7/15/2015 3:17 PM	RC File	4 KB
ueventd.sun8i.rc	7/15/2015 3:17 PM	RC File	2 KB

- **Create and change First Boot logo in Stock rom**

Here there are following steps to create and change boot log in android.

1) Extract stock rom according previous chapter and change its name from bootloader.fex to bootloader.img.

158 | Android Firmware Customization

Name	Date modified	Type	Size
_iso	7/1/2015 3:01 PM	File folder	
aultls32.fex	5/16/2015 3:17 PM	FEX File	138 KB
aultools.fex	5/16/2015 3:17 PM	FEX File	151 KB
boot.fex	5/16/2015 4:03 PM	FEX File	9,740 KB
boot0_nand.fex	5/16/2015 3:17 PM	FEX File	32 KB
boot0_sdcard.fex	5/16/2015 3:17 PM	FEX File	32 KB
bootloader.fex	5/16/2015 3:19 PM	FEX File	5,919 KB
bootloader.fex.bak	5/16/2015 3:19 PM	BAK File	5,919 KB
cardscript.fex	5/16/2015 3:17 PM	FEX File	2 KB
cardtool.fex	5/16/2015 3:17 PM	FEX File	80 KB
config.fex	5/16/2015 3:17 PM	FEX File	38 KB
diskfs.fex	5/16/2015 3:17 PM	FEX File	1 KB
dlinfo.fex	5/16/2015 3:17 PM	FEX File	16 KB
env.fex	5/16/2015 3:17 PM	FEX File	128 KB
fes1.fex	5/16/2015 3:17 PM	FEX File	7 KB
image.cfg	5/16/2015 3:17 PM	CFG File	3 KB
recovery.fex	5/16/2015 3:17 PM	FEX File	11,738 KB
split_xxxx.fex	5/16/2015 3:17 PM	FEX File	1 KB
sunxi_mbr.fex	5/16/2015 3:17 PM	FEX File	64 KB
sys_config.fex	5/16/2015 3:17 PM	FEX File	59 KB

2) Create a folder bootloder and copy bootloader.img file here.

Name	Date modified	Type	Size
bootloader.img	3/27/2015 1:37 PM	IMG File	7,421 KB

3) Install powerISO software and right on bootloader.img file and select PowerISO then Extract To.

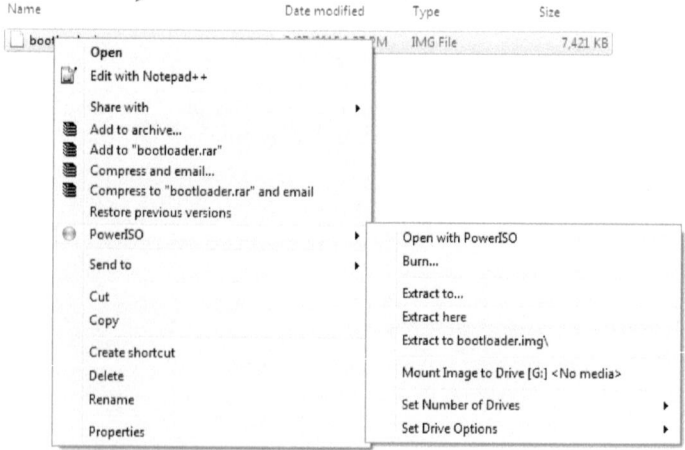

4) Here you can see file structure of bootloader.img file.

Name	Size	Type	Modified
bat		File folder	1/1/1980 12:00 AM
bootlogo.bmp	1501 KB	Bitmap image	3/27/2015 1:36 PM
data.need.backup	1 KB	BACKUP File	1/1/1980 12:00 AM
font24.sft	337 KB	SFT File	1/1/1980 12:00 AM
font32.sft	350 KB	SFT File	1/1/1980 12:00 AM
magic.bin	1 KB	BIN File	1/1/1980 12:00 AM
script.bin	38 KB	BIN File	1/1/1980 12:00 AM
script0.bin	38 KB	BIN File	1/1/1980 12:00 AM

Create a .bmp file for boot logo and Click add button to replace new boot logo then save.

- **Create and change second Boot logo in Stock rom**

Create boot logo

As we know that second boot logo in stock rom exist in form of .rle file form.

Here there are following steps to create .rle boot logo file.

1) First of all download logogen tools and extract it.

Name	Date modified	Type	Size
BmpConvert.exe	1/4/2012 5:28 PM	Application	1,663 KB
BMPConvert_UserManual.doc	1/4/2012 5:28 PM	Microsoft Office ...	64 KB

2) Copy bmp file of boot logo here.

Name	Date modified	Type	Size
BmpConvert.exe	1/4/2012 5:28 PM	Application	1,663 KB
BMPConvert_UserManual.doc	1/4/2012 5:28 PM	Microsoft Office ...	64 KB
logo.bmp	3/27/2015 1:36 PM	Bitmap image	1,501 KB

3) BmpConvert.exe file and select bmp file.

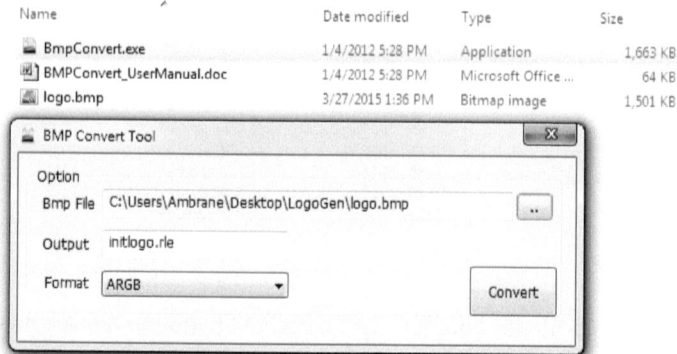

5) Press convert button it will create a .rle file for boot logo with name initlogo.rle.

Change boot logo

Here there are following steps to create .rle boot logo file.

1) Extract stock rom according previous chapter and change its name from boot.fex to boot.img.

Unit 16: Boot logo | 161

Name	Date modified	Type	Size
_iso	7/1/2015 3:01 PM	File folder	
aultls32.fex	5/16/2015 3:17 PM	FEX File	138 KB
aultools.fex	5/16/2015 3:17 PM	FEX File	151 KB
boot.fex	5/16/2015 4:03 PM	FEX File	9,740 KB
boot0_nand.fex	5/16/2015 3:17 PM	FEX File	32 KB
boot0_sdcard.fex	5/16/2015 3:17 PM	FEX File	32 KB
bootloader.fex	5/16/2015 3:19 PM	FEX File	5,919 KB
bootloader.fex.bak	5/16/2015 3:19 PM	BAK File	5,919 KB
cardscript.fex	5/16/2015 3:17 PM	FEX File	2 KB
cardtool.fex	5/16/2015 3:17 PM	FEX File	80 KB
config.fex	5/16/2015 3:17 PM	FEX File	38 KB
diskfs.fex	5/16/2015 3:17 PM	FEX File	1 KB
dlinfo.fex	5/16/2015 3:17 PM	FEX File	16 KB
env.fex	5/16/2015 3:17 PM	FEX File	128 KB
fes1.fex	5/16/2015 3:17 PM	FEX File	7 KB
image.cfg	5/16/2015 3:17 PM	CFG File	3 KB
recovery.fex	5/16/2015 3:17 PM	FEX File	11,738 KB
split_xxxx.fex	5/16/2015 3:17 PM	FEX File	1 KB
sunxi_mbr.fex	5/16/2015 3:17 PM	FEX File	64 KB
sys_config.fex	5/16/2015 3:17 PM	FEX File	59 KB

2) extract bootimg.zip put bootimg.exe and boot.img file in test folder.

Name	Date modified	Type	Size
boot.img	1/4/2014 4:08 PM	IMG File	4,566 KB
bootimg.exe	4/20/2014 6:35 AM	Application	3,920 KB

3) now go in test folder and click Ctrl+Shift and right click and choose Open command window here.

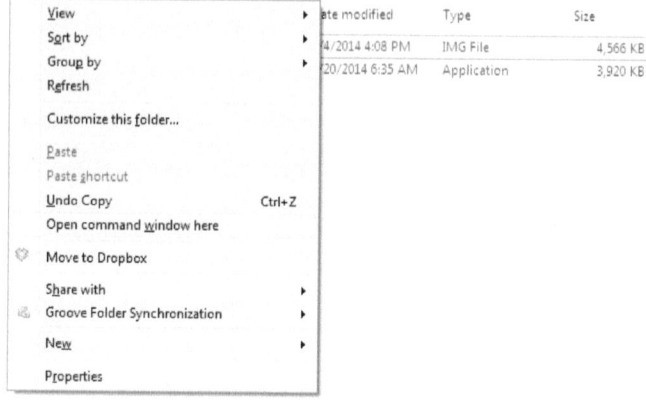

4) And write command **bootimg.exe –unpack-bootimg boot.img** and press enter

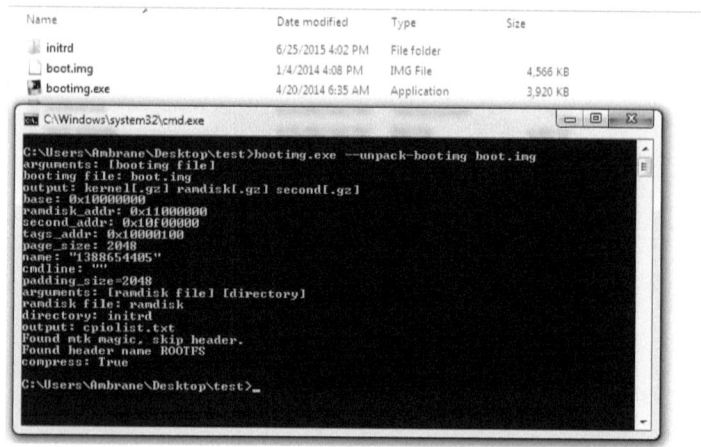

5) Open initrd folder and replace initlogo.rle file.

6) After edit rle file write command **bootimg.exe –unpack-bootimg boot.img** and press enter to again repack boot.img

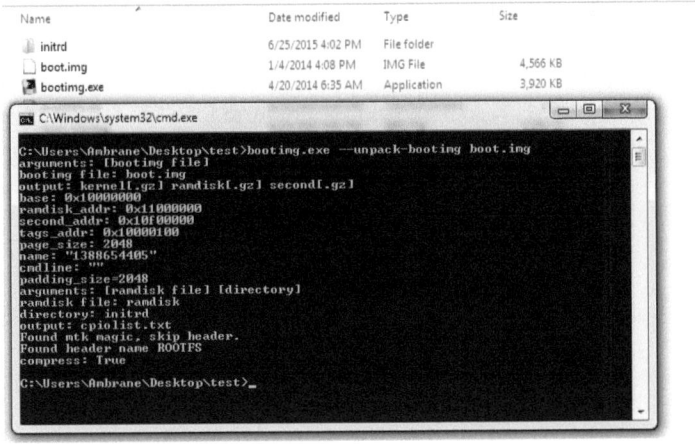

7) After edit file and folder in boot file we can Repack boot.img.

For repack boot file run this command **boot.img --repack-bootimg** And press enter.

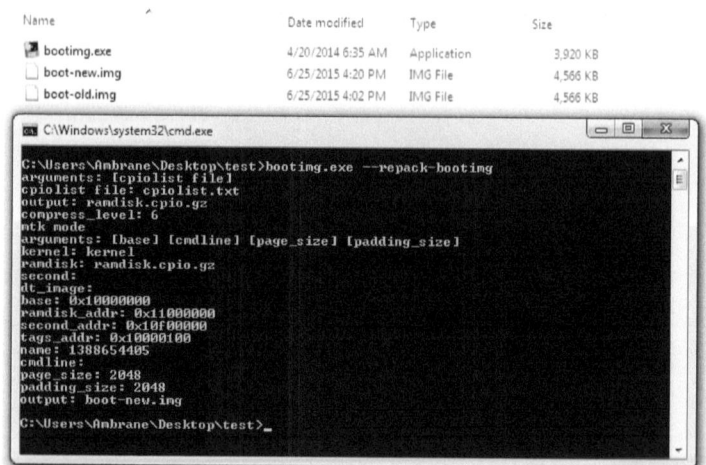

Here we get two files boot-new.img as edited boot file and boot-old.img old file.

- **boot logo in MTK rom**

There may be exist two boot logo in android stock rom.

First boot logo

First boot log in MTK rom exist in root in form logo.bin format.

Unit 16: Boot logo | 165

Name	Date modified	Type	Size
appsboot.mbn	12/3/2014 12:11 AM	MBN File	238 KB
appsboot.raw	12/3/2014 12:11 AM	RAW File	238 KB
boot.img	12/3/2014 12:10 AM	IMG File	4,136 KB
BPLGUInfoCustomAppSrcP_MT6582_S00...	12/3/2014 12:11 AM	File	5,422 KB
cache.img	12/3/2014 12:12 AM	IMG File	6,169 KB
Checksum.ini	3/26/2015 2:02 PM	Configuration sett...	1 KB
CheckSum_Gen.exe	12/3/2014 12:11 AM	Application	136 KB
clean_steps.mk	12/3/2014 12:11 AM	MK File	40 KB
custom_build_verno	12/3/2014 12:11 AM	File	1 KB
EBR1	12/3/2014 12:11 AM	File	1 KB
EBR2	12/3/2014 12:11 AM	File	1 KB
installed-files.txt	12/3/2014 12:11 AM	Text Document	86 KB
kernel	12/3/2014 12:13 AM	File	3,321 KB
kernel_mbk82_tb_kk.bin	12/3/2014 12:13 AM	BIN File	3,321 KB
lk.bin	12/3/2014 12:11 AM	BIN File	238 KB
logo.bin	12/3/2014 12:11 AM	BIN File	382 KB
MBR	12/3/2014 12:11 AM	File	1 KB
MT6582_Android_scatter.txt	12/3/2014 12:11 AM	Text Document	8 KB
preloader_mbk82_tb_kk.bin	12/3/2014 12:11 AM	BIN File	117 KB
previous_build_config.mk	12/3/2014 12:11 AM	MK File	1 KB

second boot logo

second boot log in MTK rom exist in isboot.img and path is /system/media/imagesin form boot_logo format.

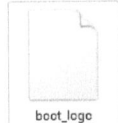

boot_logo

- **Create and change First Boot logo in MTK rom**

We already know that First boot logo in MTK rom exist in root in form logo.bin format.

So there are some steps to create and change first boot logo in android mtk rom.

1) extract Logo Builder tools and copy original logo.bin file here.

Name	Date modified	Type	Size
es	6/17/2015 5:05 PM	File folder	
it	6/17/2015 5:05 PM	File folder	
pt	6/17/2015 5:05 PM	File folder	
ru	6/17/2015 5:05 PM	File folder	
zh-Hans	6/17/2015 5:05 PM	File folder	
ignored.txt	7/22/2015 4:53 PM	Text Document	0 KB
Ionic.Zip.dll	8/7/2011 8:01 AM	Application extens...	452 KB
logo.bin	1/20/2014 2:09 PM	BIN File	249 KB
logo.exe	5/11/2014 8:25 PM	Application	9 KB
logo.exe.config	5/4/2014 2:36 PM	XML Configuratio...	1 KB
LogoBuilder.exe	5/16/2014 7:32 PM	Application	375 KB
LogoBuilder.exe.config	5/4/2014 2:36 PM	XML Configuratio...	1 KB
sizes.txt	7/22/2015 4:53 PM	Text Document	1 KB
Tips.dll	5/5/2014 9:54 PM	Application extens...	23 KB
Tips.dll.config	5/4/2014 2:29 PM	XML Configuratio...	2 KB
tips.txt	12/8/2012 6:54 PM	Text Document	2 KB

2) run logobuilder.exe

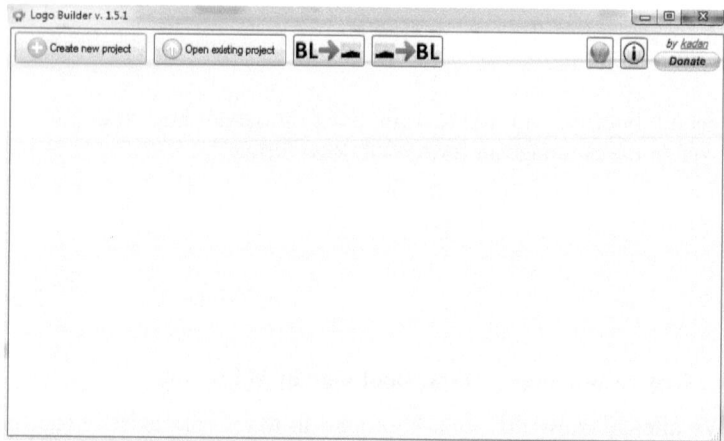

3) press create new project button and provide path of original logo.bin file and extract it in a new folder as name logo here.

Unit 16: Boot logo | 167

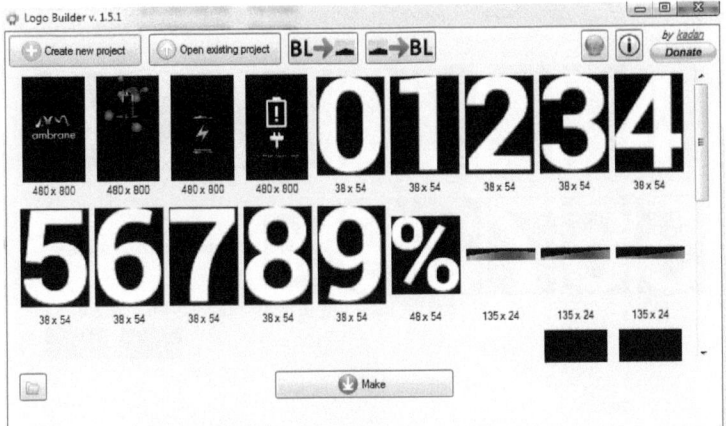

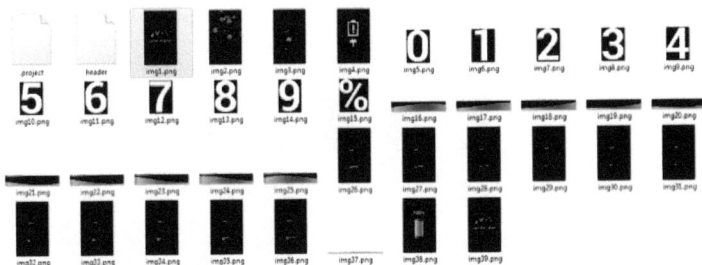

4) so create a edited logo image and replace with original image. here we replacing img1 and img39 images with new logo image.

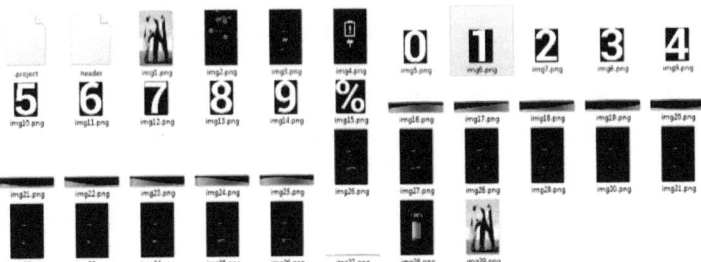

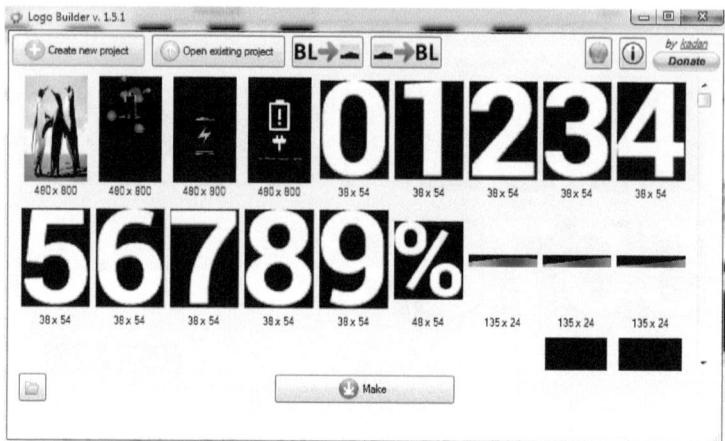

5) After replace now we can again create logo.bin file using press make button. And you can see it in logo folder.

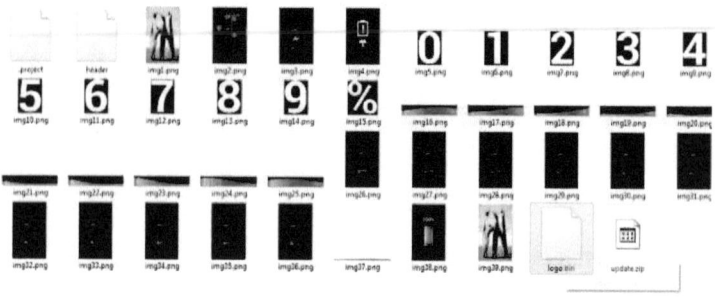

6) Replace this new logo.bin file with original logo.bin file.

- **Create and change second boot logo in MTK rom**

We already know that second boot log in MTK rom exist in isboot.img and path **is /system/media/images** in form boot_logo format.

So there are some steps to create and change second boot logo in android mtk rom

Unit 16: Boot logo | 169

1) Extract Image_Search_Editor.zip to a folder.

Name	Date modified	Type	Size
1.ACT	5/8/2006 11:04 AM	ACT File	1 KB
2bpp.act	10/26/2004 3:33 PM	ACT File	1 KB
4bpp.act	10/26/2004 3:53 PM	ACT File	1 KB
anita.act	10/26/2004 4:02 PM	ACT File	1 KB
blackbody.act	10/24/2004 2:35 PM	ACT File	1 KB
C960-504-06.lst	4/1/2007 1:53 PM	LST File	56 KB
current2.pal	2/3/2010 11:31 PM	PAL File	1 KB
current4.pal	2/3/2010 11:31 PM	PAL File	1 KB
current8.pal	2/3/2010 11:31 PM	PAL File	1 KB
grayscale.act	10/24/2004 2:35 PM	ACT File	1 KB
Image Search Editor.exe	3/18/2008 10:19 PM	Application	258 KB
Image Search Editor.ini	2/3/2010 11:31 PM	Configuration sett...	1 KB
Image Search Editor.lst	3/31/2008 1:54 PM	LST File	0 KB
macos.act	10/24/2004 2:34 PM	ACT File	1 KB
readme.txt	3/18/2008 10:13 PM	Text Document	1 KB
spectrum.act	10/24/2004 2:35 PM	ACT File	1 KB
windows.act	10/24/2004 2:34 PM	ACT File	1 KB

2) Now open Image Search Editor.exe.

170 | Android Firmware Customization

3) Select the file, boot_logo.bin to open.

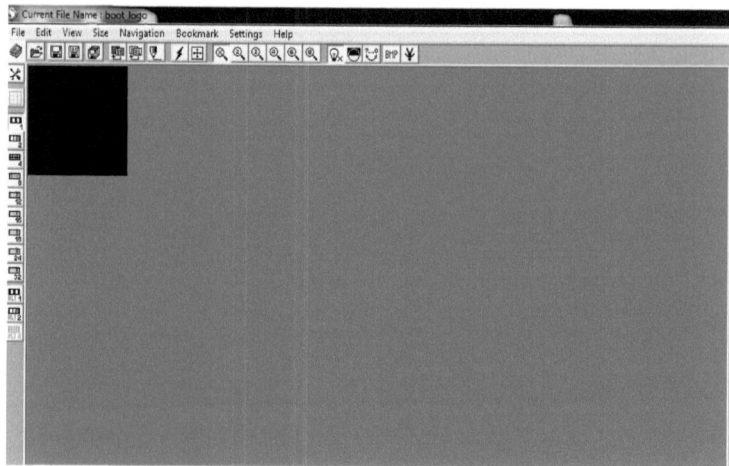

4) Now select 16 colors from the left side panel.
5) Now press BMP button on the toolbar on the top.
6) Now resize the image according your device size by press : Size --> 'Set image Size' .

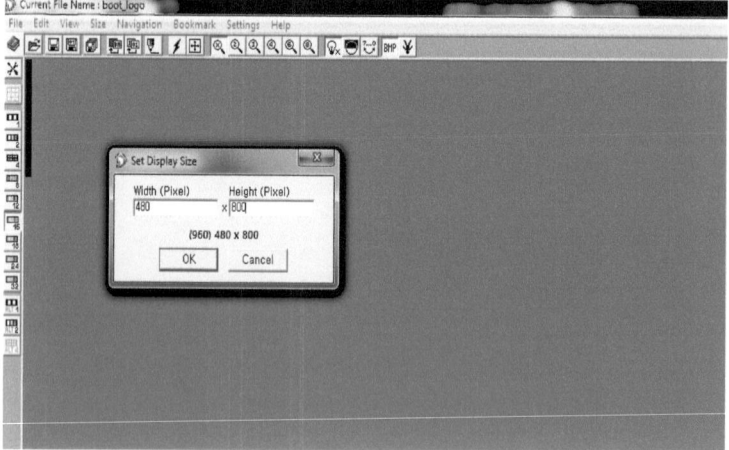

7) Press ok Now you should see the full default boot logo image.

8) Now, select: Edit-->Replace by new boot logo BMP image. Select the bmp image that you saved then press apply.

9) Then, go to File-->Save as BIN. Save it and rename this file as boot_logo.
10) Now replace this new boot_logo with original boot_logo file.

Boot logo in Rockchip Rom

We have already seen rom structure of rockchip rom. In rockchip rom It may be exit one or two boot logo.

In rockchip rom boot logo exist in form of .ppm with name logo. Here we can see it in below picture.

Name	Date modified	Type	Size
bootanimation	7/23/2015 11:12 AM	File folder	
logo.ppm	7/23/2015 11:12 AM	PPM File	2,706 KB

Create and change boot logo in rockchip rom

Now there are lot of tools which can convert a .jpg or .png image to .ppm image or we can also convert online it .

Here we will see how we can change boot logo in rockchip rom.

There are following steps to extract rockchip rom and change boot logo.

1) extract factory tool and copy rockchip rom here.

Name	Date modified	Type	Size
FactoryToolV4.4	7/11/2015 8:22 AM	File folder	
FactoryToolV4.4	2/3/2015 1:38 PM	WinRAR archive	11,512 KB
new.img	2/3/2015 3:15 PM	IMG File	713,708 KB

2) run FWFactoryTool

Name	Date modified	Type	Size
bin	3/11/2014 3:15 PM	File folder	
config	3/11/2014 3:03 PM	File folder	
Doc	3/11/2014 3:03 PM	File folder	
Language	3/11/2014 3:03 PM	File folder	
Log	6/17/2014 1:23 AM	File folder	
Output	6/9/2014 12:40 AM	File folder	
Plugin	3/11/2014 3:04 PM	File folder	
config	6/9/2014 12:41 AM	Configuration sett...	1 KB
FWFactoryTool	3/11/2014 3:03 PM	Application	524 KB

Unit 16: Boot logo | 173

3) Provide path of rockchip rom image file.

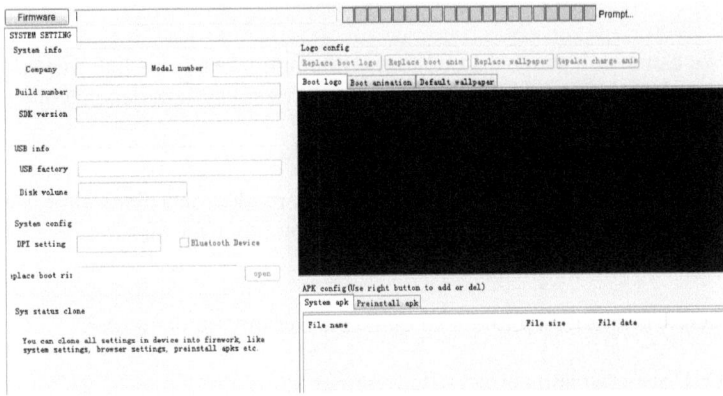

4) In tempFolder we can see logo.ppm file exist so now we can replace with our custom logo.ppm file.

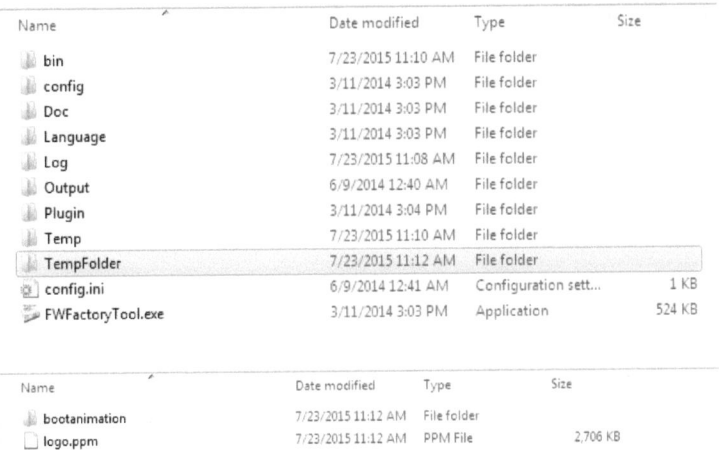

Unit 17 : Install android rom

We can install android stock rom with mainly two tools like live suit and phoenix but both are platform or operating system dependent.

- **Install device driver**

Now at this time lot of rom available in market and many time we will need those driver to connect with computer for installation rom or may other reason.

Here following step to install device driver in your computer.

1) Download and extract usb diver.zip

Name	Date modified	Type	Size
amd64	7/1/2015 3:28 PM	File folder	
i386	7/1/2015 3:28 PM	File folder	
android_winusb.inf	9/20/2014 3:04 AM	Setup Information	6 KB
androidwinusb86.cat	9/20/2014 3:04 AM	Security Catalog	11 KB
androidwinusba64.cat	9/20/2014 3:04 AM	Security Catalog	11 KB
source.properties	9/20/2014 3:04 AM	PROPERTIES File	17 KB

2) Firstly right click on my computer->manage->device manger

Here you can see that if your device does not install in computer it show unknown device.

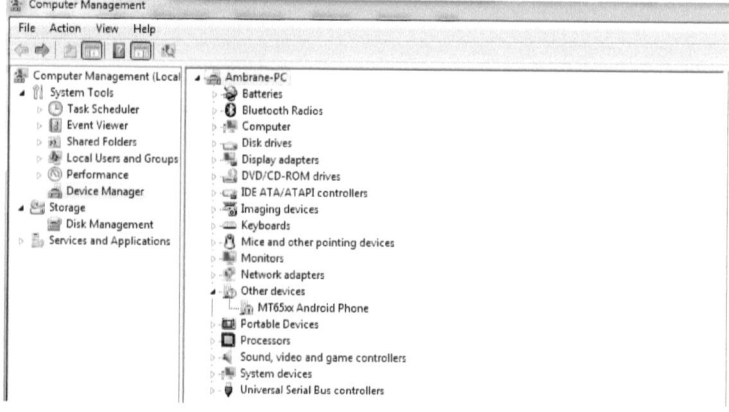

Unit 17: Install android rom | 175

3) Right click on unknown device.

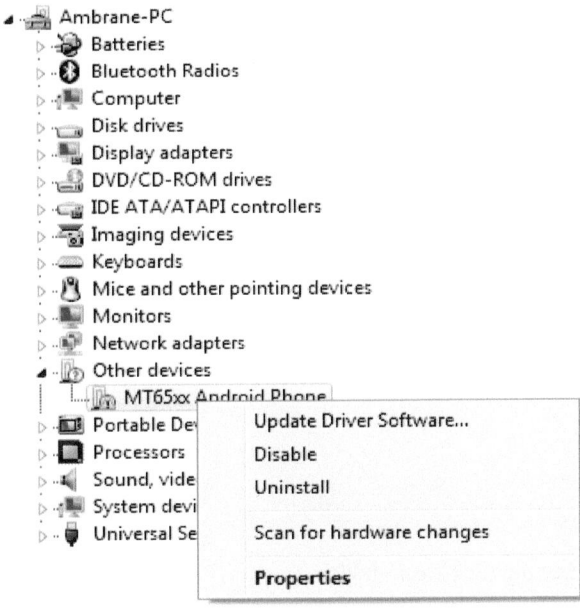

4) Click on Update Driver Software.

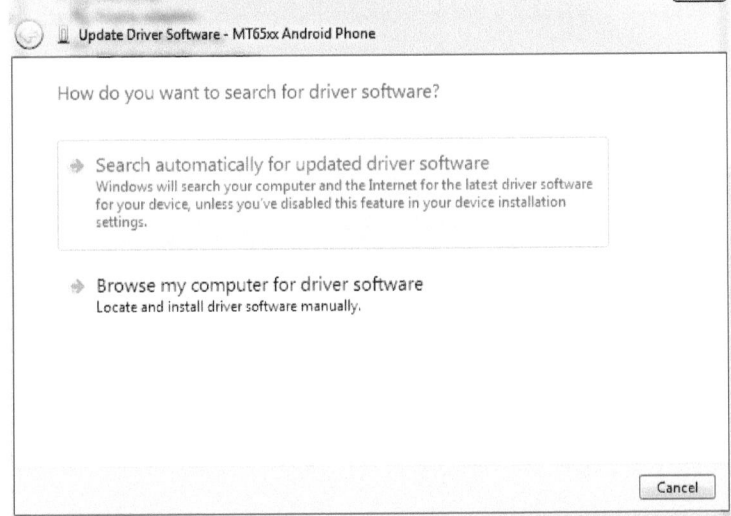

176 | Android Firmware Customization

5) Click on browse my computer for driver software.

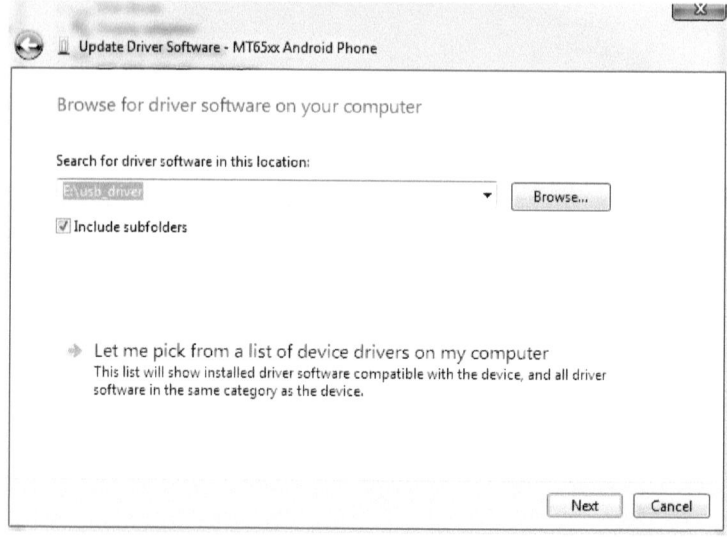

6) Click on Let me pick from device.

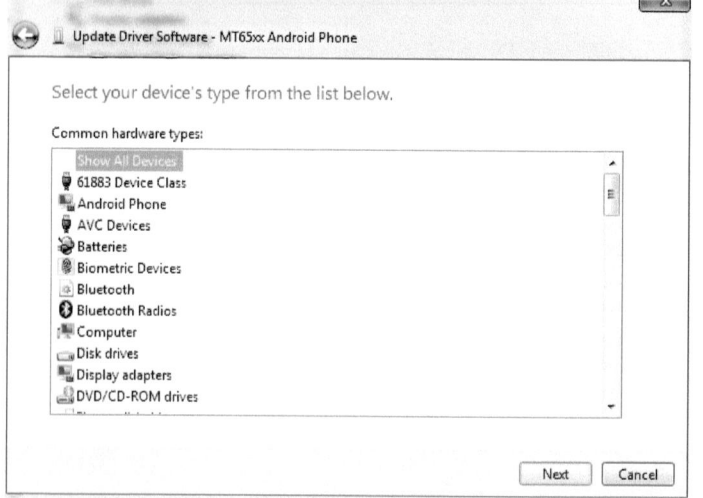

Unit 17: Install android rom | 177

7) Press next button.

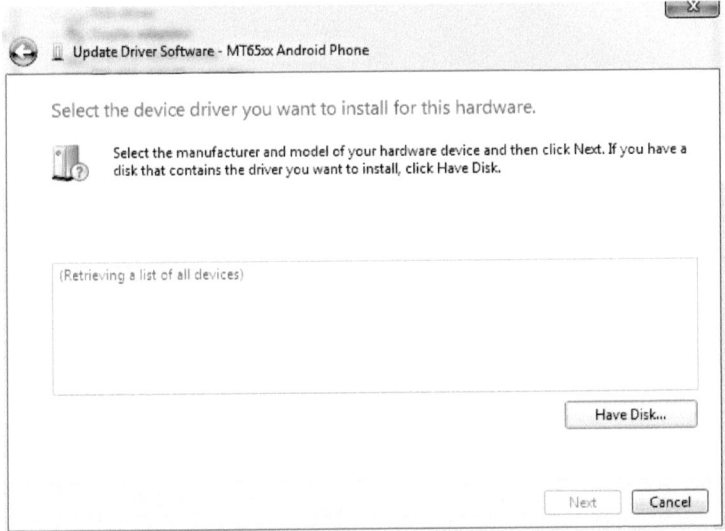

8) Then press Have Disk button.

178 | Android Firmware Customization

9) Provide android_winusb.inf file path by select browse button and press ok button.

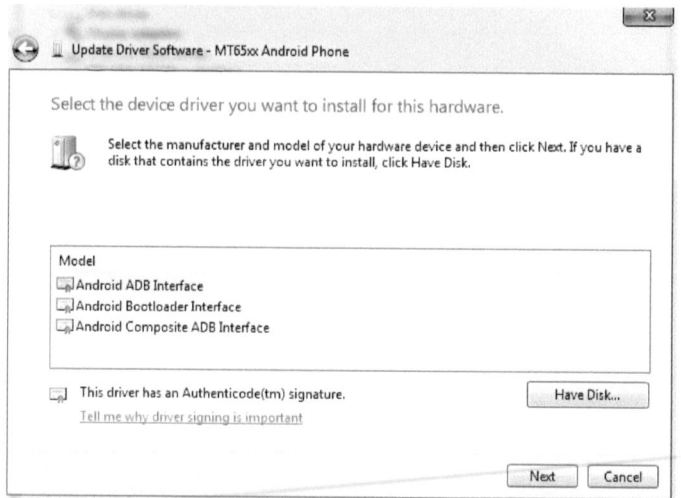

10) Select android adb interface and click next button.

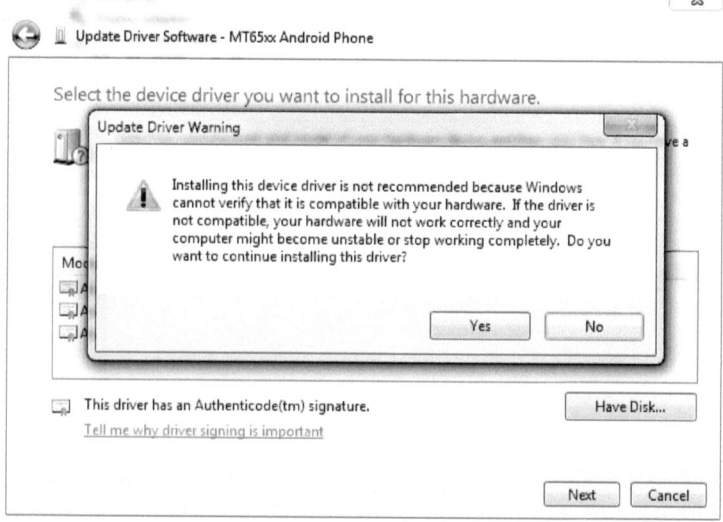

Unit 17: Install android rom | 179

11) Then press yes button and it will install adb driver for device.

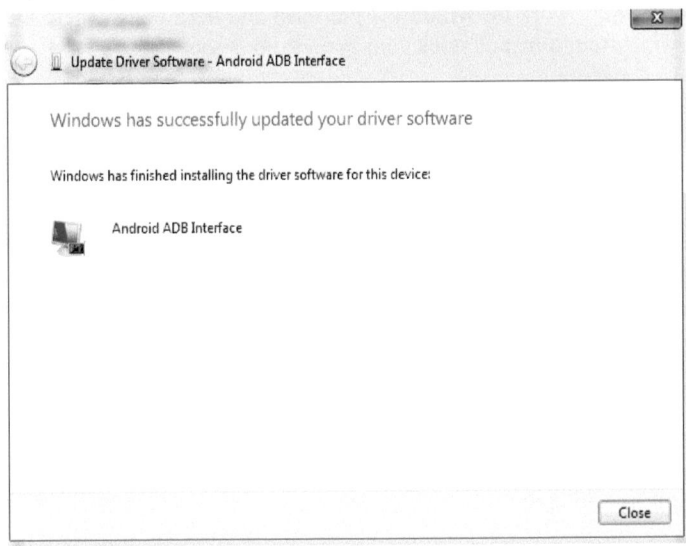

12) You can see install driver for your device.

• Install stock rom by live suit tool

This tool may work on window 7 platform and here below there are following step to install stock rom in android device.

1) Download and install android adb drivers on your computer.

2) Download and extract livesuite.zip file on your computer.

3) Run livesuit.exe

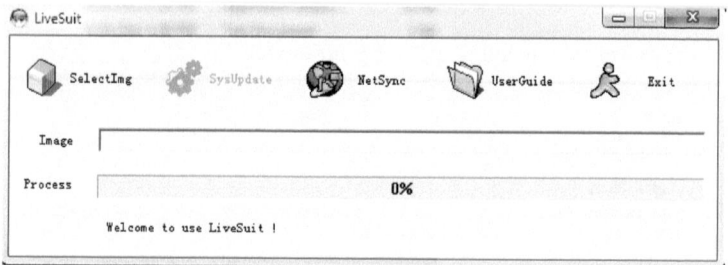

4) Select stock rom path by press SelectImg.

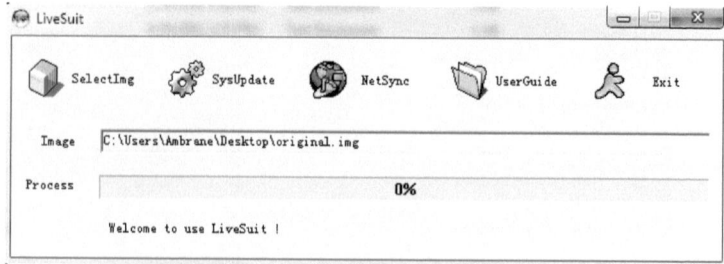

Unit 17: Install android rom | 181

5) Now we can connect android Smartphone or tablet with computer using usb cable and it should be power off.

   Before connect your device press volume down button and connect your device with computer with usb cable while holding volume down button press power button around 10 times.

6) After successfully reorganization to your device we get a window to format your device and press yes.

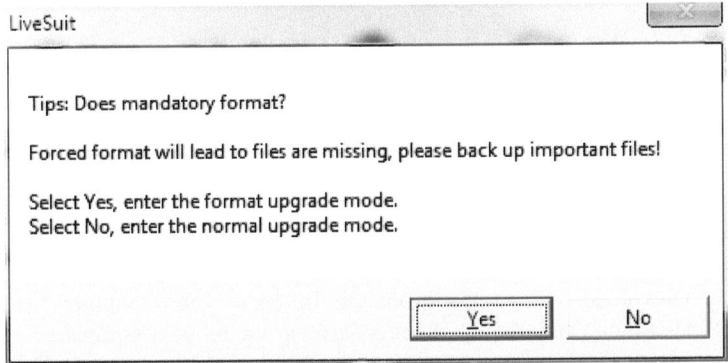

7) Again we will get other window, press yes again the it will automatically start to installation rom in your device.

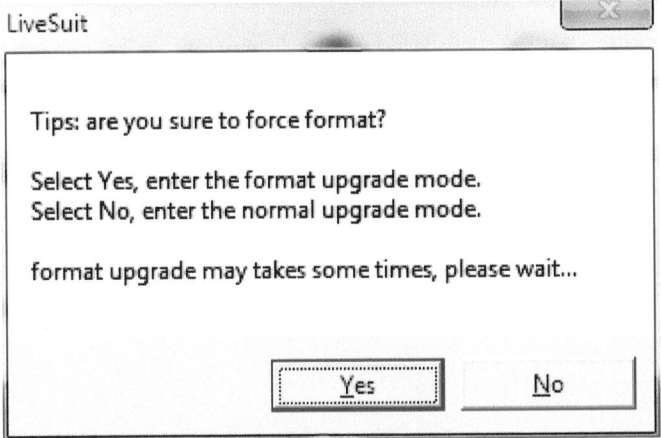

8) After successfully installation software we will get upgrade window.

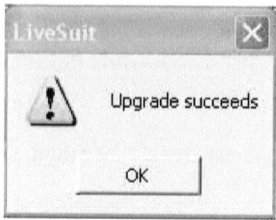

- **Install stock rom by phoenix Card tool**

Install with phoenix card dependent on os platform. it may be install software on window 7 or may be on window xp by phoenix card tools. It depend on version of phoenix card version.

here below there are following step to install stock rom in android device.
1) Download and install android adb drivers on your computer.
2) Download and extract phoenixCard.zip file on your computer.
3) Insert TF Card /MicroSD Card in Card reader and attach Card Reader with PC. Use minimum 1GB memory card.
4) format MicroSD card to make sure it does not have any other file or its not corrupted.
5) Open PhoenixCard.exe

Name	Date modified	Type	Size
Diskinfo.dll	3/11/2010 12:36 PM	Application extens...	36 KB
DynamicData.dll	11/24/2011 2:47 PM	Application extens...	60 KB
FsOp.dll	12/9/2011 11:50 AM	Application extens...	156 KB
FsOp2.dll	11/2/2011 5:12 PM	Application extens...	152 KB
fstool.dll	7/29/2011 4:32 PM	Application extens...	768 KB
help	2/1/2012 1:50 PM	PDF File	161 KB
ImageOps.dll	10/25/2011 6:54 PM	Application extens...	40 KB
ImgDecode.dll	10/25/2011 6:54 PM	Application extens...	44 KB
IniParasPtg.dll	11/22/2011 7:42 PM	Application extens...	44 KB
Langplg.dll	8/16/2011 4:40 PM	Application extens...	229 KB
Modify	10/25/2011 6:54 PM	Configuration sett...	1 KB
ParserManager.dll	2/29/2012 4:47 PM	Application extens...	64 KB
PhoenixCard	3/2/2012 11:22 AM	Application	100 KB
PhoenixCard	6/11/2012 5:43 PM	Configuration sett...	9 KB
PhoenixCard-TE+IS-¤	2/1/2012 1:51 PM	Microsoft Word 9...	117 KB
PhoenixCard-TE+IS-¤	11/11/2011 11:45 ...	PDF File	108 KB
PlgVector.dll	7/28/2011 3:34 PM	Application extens...	68 KB
PlugInMgr.dll	5/11/2010 12:36 PM	Application extens...	44 KB
proxypid1_solution_net_141516D2-BAC7-...	12/26/2012 10:23 ...	KEY File	4 KB
Single.dll	10/25/2011 6:54 PM	Application extens...	92 KB

6) click on Diskcheck .Disk Check will detect TF Card port Like J Drive , Kdrive.

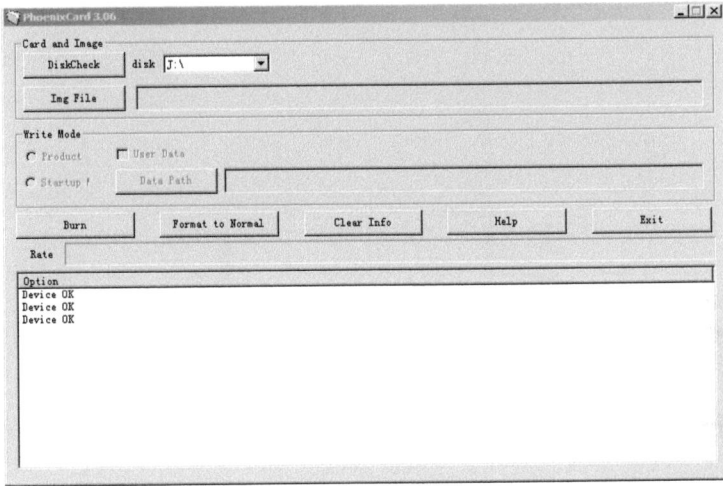

7) Now click on Img File button and browse stock rom file from the above extracted directory.

184 | Android Firmware Customization

8) Then click on Format to Normal button to format the sdcard using this application.

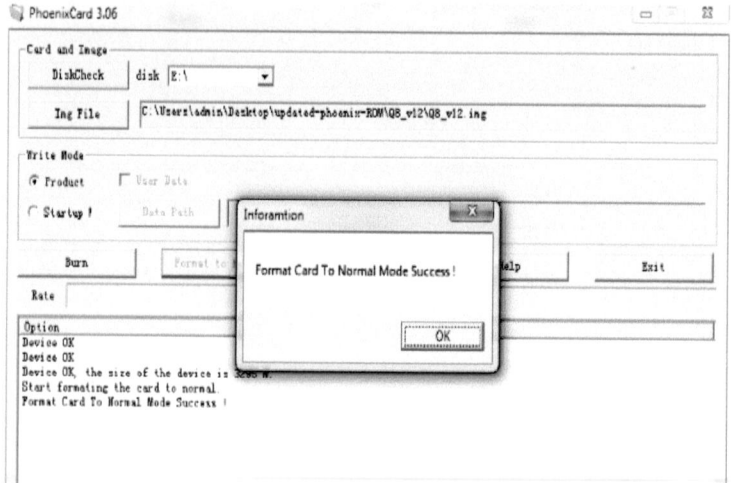

9) Finally click Burn button to start burning an image to Micro-SD card.

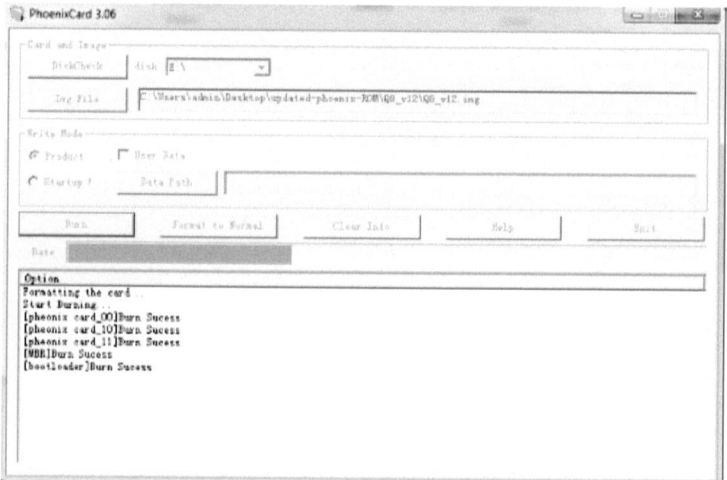

Unit 17: Install android rom | 185

10) Wait until the Burn End.. message appears on the screen.

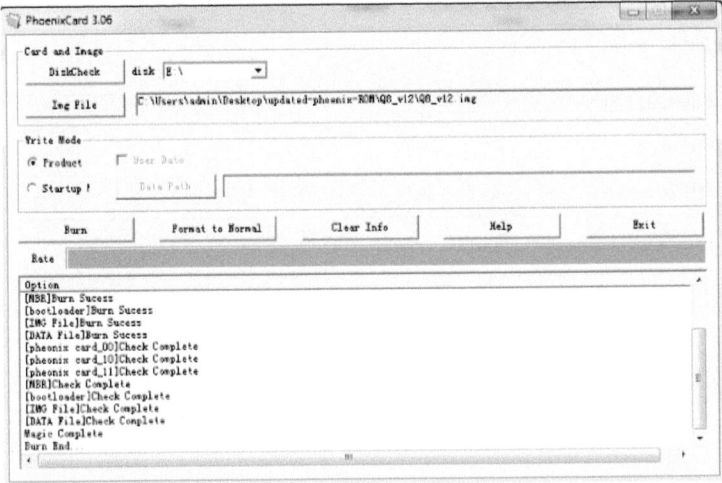

11) Switch off your device and insert memory card in it and switch on the device. Rom will be start installation automatically and after 100% complete remove your memory card in and start your device.

- **Install MTK rom by Sp flash tool**

here below there are following step to install MTK rom in android device.
1) Download and install android adb drivers on your computer.
2) Download and extract Sp Flash tool.zip file on your computer.

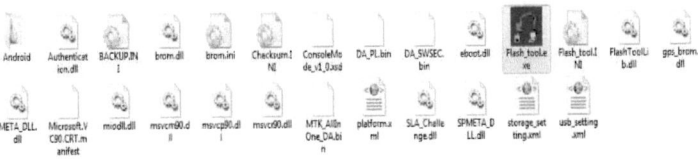

186 | Android Firmware Customization

3) Run flashtool.exe file.

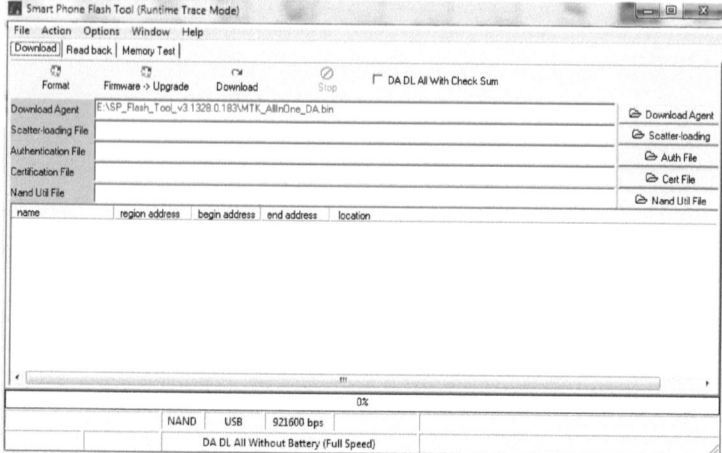

4) Provide rom Android_scatter.txt file path by Press Scatter-loading File button.

cache.img	12/3/2014 12:12 AM	IMG File	6,169 KB
Checksum.ini	3/26/2015 2:02 PM	Configuration sett...	1 KB
CheckSum_Gen.exe	12/3/2014 12:11 AM	Application	136 KB
clean_steps.mk	12/3/2014 12:11 AM	MK File	40 KB
custom_build_verno	12/3/2014 12:11 AM	File	1 KB
EBR1	12/3/2014 12:11 AM	File	1 KB
EBR2	12/3/2014 12:11 AM	File	1 KB
installed-files.txt	12/3/2014 12:11 AM	Text Document	86 KB
kernel	12/3/2014 12:13 AM	File	3,321 KB
kernel_mbk82_tb_kk.bin	12/3/2014 12:13 AM	BIN File	3,321 KB
lk.bin	12/3/2014 12:11 AM	BIN File	238 KB
logo.bin	12/3/2014 12:11 AM	BIN File	382 KB
MBR	12/3/2014 12:11 AM	File	1 KB
MT6582_Android_scatter.txt	12/3/2014 12:11 AM	Text Document	8 KB
preloader_mbk82_tb_kk.bin	12/3/2014 12:11 AM	BIN File	117 KB
previous_build_config.mk	12/3/2014 12:11 AM	MK File	1 KB
ramdisk.img	12/3/2014 12:11 AM	IMG File	811 KB
ramdisk-recovery.img	12/3/2014 12:14 AM	IMG File	1,187 KB
recovery.img	12/3/2014 12:14 AM	IMG File	4,512 KB
secro.img	12/3/2014 12:11 AM	IMG File	132 KB
system.img	12/11/2014 1:07 AM	IMG File	851,611 KB
system.tmp	12/3/2014 12:27 AM	TMP File	141,392 KB
userdata.img	12/3/2014 1:52 AM	IMG File	17,885 KB

Unit 17: Install android rom | 187

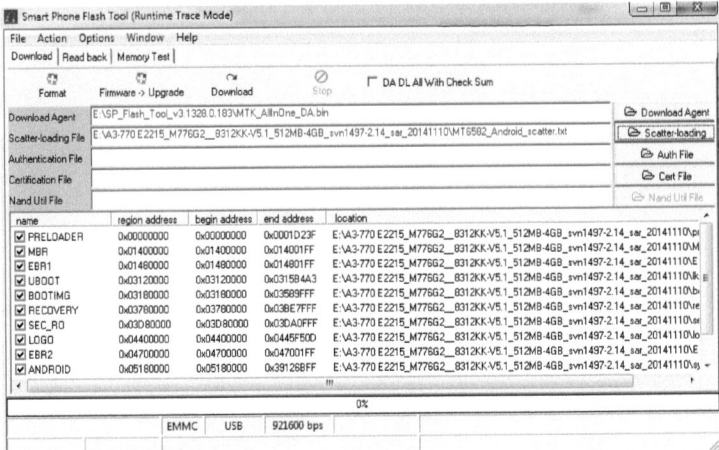

5) Press F9 or download button.

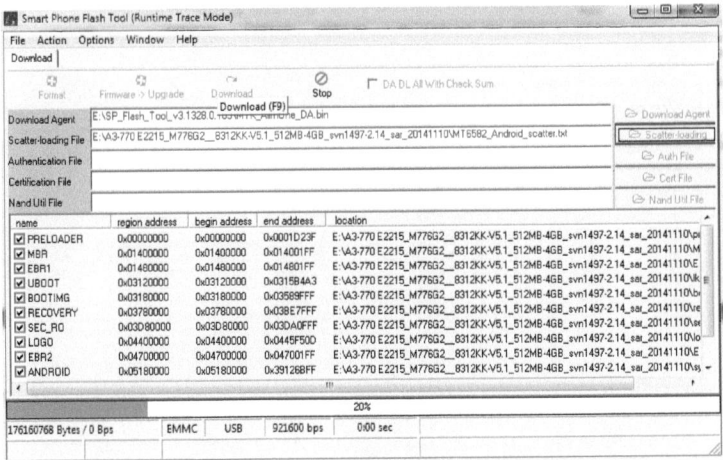

6) Connect your device to computer using usb cable. It will start format first by red line and then it will start install software by yellow line.

188 | Android Firmware Customization

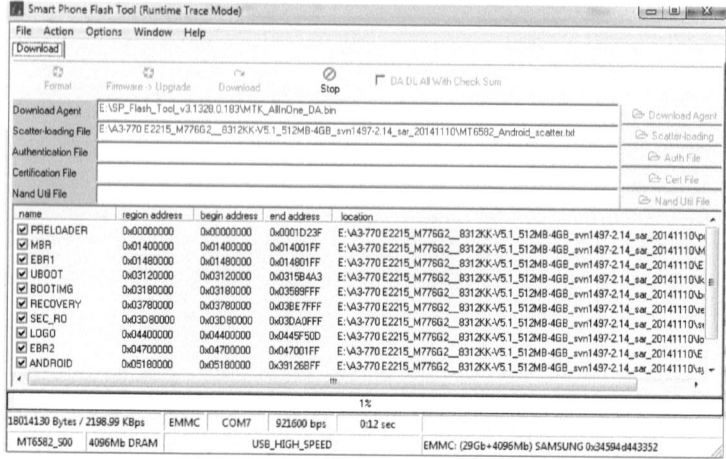

7) After complete 100% it will install successfully.

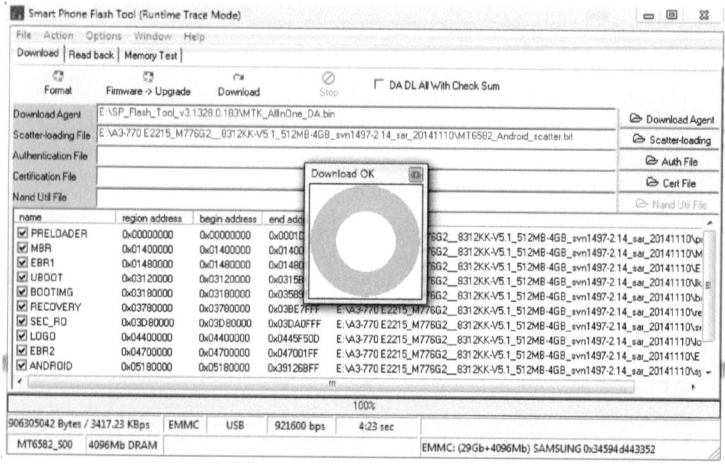

8) Then remove usb cable and now it install rom.

- **Install Rockchip rom by batch tool**

here below there are following step to install Rockchip rom in android device.

1) Download and install android adb drivers on your computer.

Unit 17: Install android rom | 189

2) Download and extract batch tool.zip file on your computer.

Name	Date modified	Type	Size
Language	4/29/2015 3:49 PM	File folder	
Log	4/29/2015 3:49 PM	File folder	
RockusbDriver_3066	4/29/2015 3:49 PM	File folder	
UID	4/8/2015 3:17 PM	File folder	
config.ini	5/9/2014 2:26 PM	Configuration sett...	4 KB
RKBatchTool.exe	9/9/2014 4:03 PM	Application	929 KB
sdf.doc	3/5/2012 5:48 PM	Microsoft Office ...	249 KB

3) Run RKBatch Tool.exe.

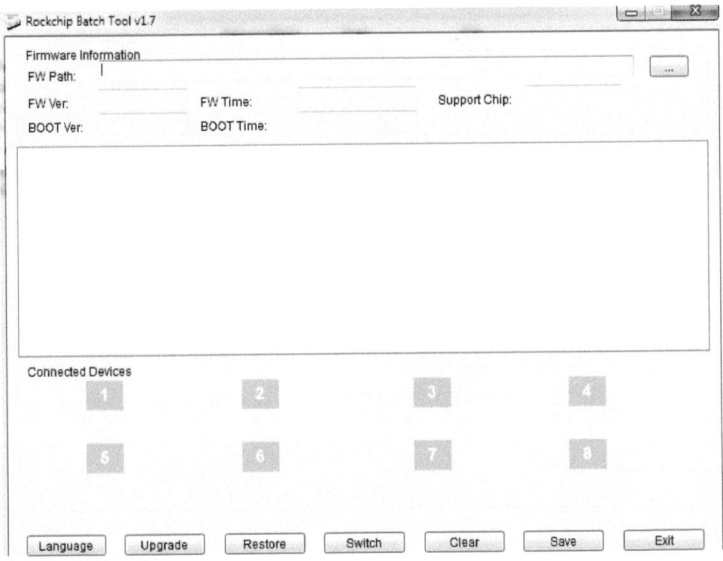

190 | Android Firmware Customization

4) Provide rockchip rom path by browsing.

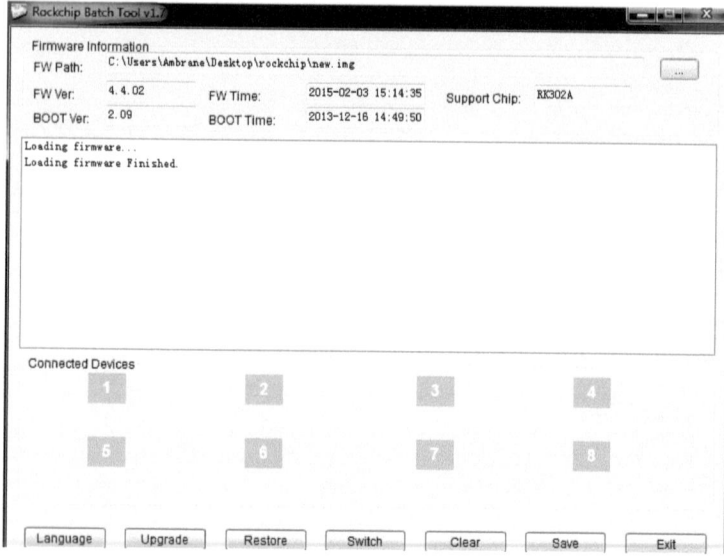

5) Connect your device with computer by usb cable with press power and volume up key simultaneously.

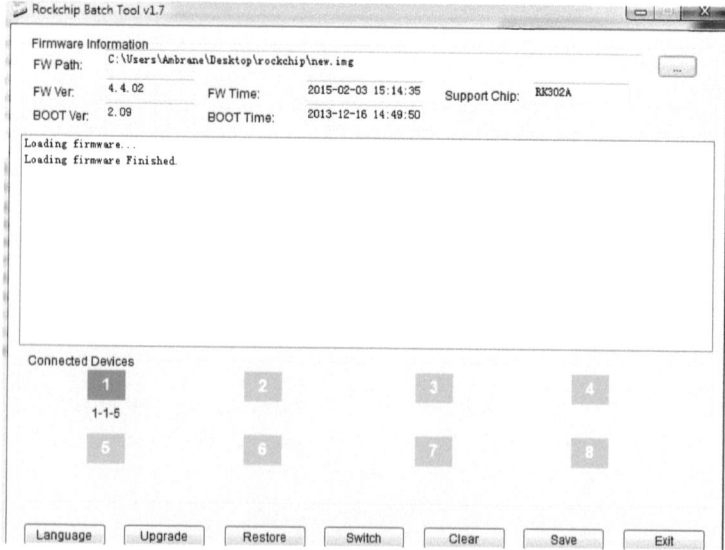

Unit 17: Install android rom | 191

6) Then press upgrade button the start to install rom in device after 100% remove cable form derive and device ready to use with new firmware.

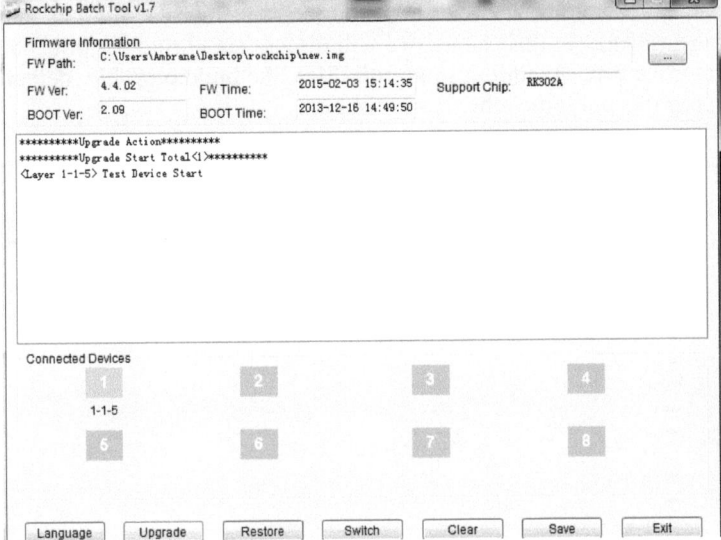

Unit 18: Other Customization

We already know that how we can extract any types rom how we can do customize it because customize rom improve android rom performance. In this chapter we will discuss about rom performance improvement by editing some rom files like build.prop file, default .prop file and some other customization.

- **Build.prop file**

Basically build.prop is system or firmware properties file which is located in /system folder. System Directory consists of all necessary information for your rom specific build.

Name	Date modified	Type	Size
app	7/22/2015 4:33 PM	File folder	
bin	7/22/2015 4:33 PM	File folder	
data	7/22/2015 4:33 PM	File folder	
etc	7/22/2015 4:33 PM	File folder	
fonts	7/22/2015 4:33 PM	File folder	
framework	7/22/2015 4:33 PM	File folder	
lib	7/22/2015 4:33 PM	File folder	
lost+found	7/22/2015 4:33 PM	File folder	
media	7/22/2015 4:33 PM	File folder	
mobile_toolkit	7/22/2015 4:33 PM	File folder	
res	7/22/2015 4:33 PM	File folder	
tts	7/22/2015 4:33 PM	File folder	
usr	7/22/2015 4:33 PM	File folder	
vendor	7/22/2015 4:33 PM	File folder	
xbin	7/22/2015 4:33 PM	File folder	
build.prop	7/22/2015 4:33 PM	PROP File	4 KB

We are going to edit this file and many custom ROM developers edit these files to free up existing RAM. Editing should be carefully done and once small changes can be harmful to your mobile device. Back up all your data before you make any changes.

1) **Fast Reboot**
    persist.sys.purgeable_assets=1

2) **Faster boot**
    ro.config.hw_quickpoweron=true

3) **Increasing Video Recording Quality**
    ro.media.enc.hprof.vid.bps=8000000

4) **Change Screen Rotate To 270 degree**
   windowsmgr.support_rotation_270=true;

5) **change Heap Size**
   dalvik.vm.heapsize=64m

6) **Render UI With GPU**
   debug.sf.hw=1

7) **Make device much Smoother**
   windowsmgr.max_events_per_sec=150

8) **Video Acceleration Enabled And HW debugging.**
   video.accelerate.hw=1
   debug.sf.hw=1
   debug.performance.tuning=1
   debug.egl.profiler=1 (Measure rendering time in adb shell dumpsys gfxinfo)
   debug.egl.hw=1
   debug.composition.type=gpu (Disable hardware overlays)

9) **Increase Performance**
   debug.performance.tuning=1

10) **Disable Sending Usage Data**
    ro.config.nocheckin=1

11) **Deeper Sleep/Better battery life**
    ro.ril.disable.power.collapse=1
    pm.sleep_mode=1

12) **Ringing Will Start Immediately**
    ro.telephony.call_ring.delay=0
    ring.delay=0

13) **Enable/Disable Error Checking**
    ro.kernel.android.checkjni=0

14) **change Media Streaming Quality**
    media.stagefright.enable-player=true
    media.stagefright.enable-meta=true
    media.stagefright.enable-scan=true
    media.stagefright.enable-http=true
    media.stagefright.enable-rtsp=true
    media.stagefright.enable-record=false

15) **Enable/Disable Boot Animation**
    debug.sf.nobootanimation=1

16) **Force To Remain Launcher In Memory**
    ro.HOME_APP_ADJ=1

17) **Enable/Disable Waking by Volume Buttons**
    ro.config.hwfeature_wakeupkey=0

18) **Off The Proximity Quickly After Call**
    mot.proximity.delay=25
    ro.lge.proximity.delay=25

19) **Better Signal Tweaks**
    ro.ril.hsxpa=2
    ro.ril.gprsclass=10
    ro.ril.hep=1
    ro.ril.enable.dtm=1
    ro.ril.hsdpa.category=10
    ro.ril.enable.a53=1
    ro.ril.enable.3g.prefix=1
    ro.ril.htcmaskw1.bitmask=4294967295
    ro.ril.htcmaskw1=14449
    ro.ril.hsupa.category=5
    persist.cust.tel.eons=1
    ro.config.hw_fast_dormancy=1

20) **NetSpeed Tweaks**
    net.tcp.buffersize.default=4096,87380,256960,4096,16384,256960
    net.tcp.buffersize.wifi=4096,87380,256960,4096,16384,256960
    net.tcp.buffersize.umts=4096,87380,256960,4096,16384,256960
    net.tcp.buffersize.gprs=4096,87380,256960,4096,16384,256960
    net.tcp.buffersize.edge=4096,87380,256960,4096,16384,256960

21) **Google DNS Tweak**
    net.rmnet0.dns1=8.8.8.8
    net.rmnet0.dns2=8.8.4.4
    net.dns1=8.8.8.8
    net.dns2=8.8.4.4

Unit 18: Other Customization | 195

22) **Photo And Video Quality**
    ro.media.enc.jpeg.quality=100
    ro.media.dec.jpeg.memcap=8000000
    ro.media.enc.hprof.vid.bps=8000000
    ro.media.capture.maxres=8m
    ro.media.panorama.defres=3264x1840
    ro.media.panorama.frameres=1280x720
    ro.camcorder.videoModes=true
    ro.media.enc.hprof.vid.fps=65

23) **change Touch Responsiveness**
    debug.performance.tuning=1
    video.accelerate.hw=1

24) **Scrolling Responsiveness**
    windowsmgr.max_events_per_sec=500

25) **Power Save Tweaks**
    pm.sleep_mode=1
    ro.ril.power_collapse=1
    wifi.supplicant_scan_interval=180
    ro.mot.eri.losalert.delay=1000 (could brake tethering)

26) **Enable/Disables Debug Icon On Status Bar**
    persist.adb.notify=0

27) **Faster Scrolling**
    ro.max.fling_velocity=12000
    ro.min.fling_velocity=8000
    windowsmgr.max_events_per_sec=150
    ro.min_pointer_dur=8

28) **wifi to scan less frequently**
    wifi.supplicant_scan_interval=180

29) **improve battery under no signal**
    ro.mot.eri.losalert.delay=1000

30) **makes apps load faster and frees ram**
    dalvik.vm.dexopt-flags=m=v,o=y

31) **Off The Proximity Quickly After Call**
    ro.lge.proximity.delay=25
    mot.proximity.delay=25

32) **Enable/Disables built in error reporting**
    profiler.force_disable_err_rpt=1
    profiler.force_disable_ulog=1

33) **3G Network tweaks.**
    ro.ril.hep=0
    ro.ril.hsxpa=2
    ro.ril.gprsclass=12
    ro.ril.enable.dtm=1
    ro.ril.hsdpa.category=8
    ro.ril.enable.a53=1
    ro.ril.enable.3g.prefix=1
    ro.ril.htcmaskw1.bitmask=4294967295
    ro.ril.htcmaskw1=14449
    ro.ril.hsupa.category=6

34) **Enable/Disables logcat**
    logcat.live=disable

35) **Screen recognizes only two fingers.**
    ro.product.multi_touch_enabled=true
    ro.product.max_num_touch=2

36) **Support for ipv4 and ipv6.**
    persist.telephony.support.ipv6=1
    persist.telephony.support.ipv4=1

37) **Enable/Disables blackscreen issue after a call.**
    ro.lge.proximity.delay=25
    mot.proximity.delay=25

38) **Better call voice quality.**
    ro.ril.enable.amr.wideband=1

39) **Dalvik Virtual Machine tweaks.**
    dalvik.vm.checkjni=false
    dalvik.vm.dexopt-data-only=1
    dalvik.vm.heapstartsize=5m
    dalvik.vm.heapgrowthlimit=48m
    dalvik.vm.heapsize=64m
    dalvik.vm.verify-bytecode=false
    dalvik.vm.execution-mode=int:jit
    dalvik.vm.lockprof.threshold=250
    dalvik.vm.dexopt-flags=m=v,o=y

dalvik.vm.stack-trace-file=/data/anr/traces.txt
dalvik.vm.jmiopts=forcecopy

40) **Enable/Disable notification while adb is active**
persist.adb.notify=0

41) **Change LCD density**
ro.sf.lcd.density=240

42) **Key lights stay on while screen is on.**
ro.mot.buttonlight.timeout=0

43) **Enable/Disable notification sound for SD storage insert**
persist.service.mount.playsnd=0

44) **Enable display dithering**
persist.sys.use_dithering=1

45) **change volume steps in call.**
ro.config.vc_call_steps=20

46) **Lock app in memory.**
sys.keep_app_1=com.your.app.app

47) **Enables MTP mode.**
persist.sys.usb.config=mtp

48) **Smooth Ui**
persist.service.lgospd.enable=0
persist.service.pcsync.enable=0

49) **Wireless Tweaks**
net.ipv4.ip_no_pmtu_disc=0
net.ipv4.route.flush=1
net.ipv4.tcp_ecn=0
net.ipv4.tcp_fack=1
net.ipv4.tcp_mem=187000 187000 187000
net.ipv4.tcp_moderate_rcvbuf=1
net.ipv4.tcp_no_metrics_save=1
net.ipv4.tcp_rfc1337=1
net.ipv4.tcp_rmem=4096 39000 187000
net.ipv4.tcp_sack=1
net.ipv4.tcp_timestamps=1
net.ipv4.tcp_window_scaling=1
net.ipv4.tcp_wmem=4096 39000 18700

wifi.supplicant_scan_interval=180

50) Change android device name and version
ro.build.display.id=Your ROM name
ro.build.version.release=4.4.2 (Android version)

- **Defalt.prop file**

Default.prop file is also specified android rom properties and it is located in init folder both boot.img as well as recovery.img file. This is also consists of all necessary information for your rom specific build.

ro.secure=0 it means adbd running as root by default. ro.debuggable=1 and service.adb.root=1 will allow you to run adbd as root via the adb root command.

Once you are able to run adb as root via adb root, you will be able to remount the /system/ directory as writable and can install anything which you want.

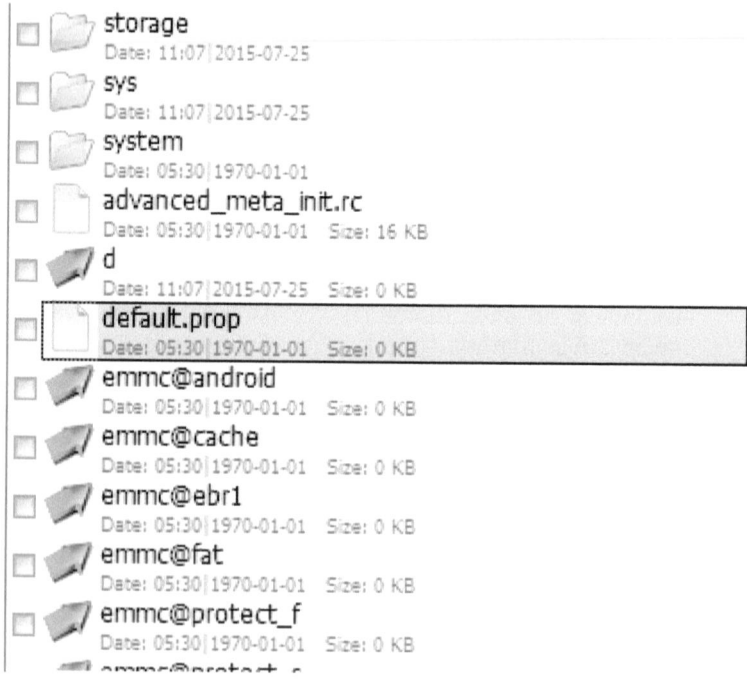

```
1  #
2  # ADDITIONAL_DEFAULT_PROPERTIES
3  #
4  ro.secure=1
5  ro.allow.mock.location=0
6  persist.mtk.aee.aed=on
7  ro.debuggable=0
8  persist.sys.usb.config=mass_storage
9  persist.service.acm.enable=0
10 ro.mount.fs=EXT4
```

1) **Root/Unroot rom**
   ro.secure=1(1 unroot,0 root)

2) **Usb Enable/Disable**
   ro.debuggable=0

3) **Storage**
   persist.sys.usb.config=mass_storage

4) **Adb enable/disable**
   persist.service.adb.enable=1

- **Add and Remove system apps**

All System applications are store in system/app directory. We from this folder we can add any application as system application and also remove.

Some application may be in system/private app or system/vendor/app directory.

Name	Date modified	Type	Size
app	7/22/2015 4:33 PM	File folder	
bin	7/22/2015 4:33 PM	File folder	
data	7/22/2015 4:33 PM	File folder	
etc	7/22/2015 4:33 PM	File folder	
fonts	7/22/2015 4:33 PM	File folder	
framework	7/22/2015 4:33 PM	File folder	
lib	7/22/2015 4:33 PM	File folder	
lost+found	7/22/2015 4:33 PM	File folder	
media	7/22/2015 4:33 PM	File folder	
mobile_toolkit	7/22/2015 4:33 PM	File folder	
res	7/22/2015 4:33 PM	File folder	
tts	7/22/2015 4:33 PM	File folder	
usr	7/22/2015 4:33 PM	File folder	
vendor	7/22/2015 4:33 PM	File folder	
xbin	7/22/2015 4:33 PM	File folder	
build.prop	7/22/2015 4:33 PM	PROP File	4 KB

Name	Date modified	Type	Size
3Dwallpaper.apk	7/22/2015 4:33 PM	APK File	672 KB
AdupsFota.apk	7/22/2015 4:33 PM	APK File	211 KB
AdupsFotaReboot.apk	7/22/2015 4:33 PM	APK File	16 KB
ApplicationGuide.apk	7/22/2015 4:33 PM	APK File	1,646 KB
ApplicationGuide.odex	7/22/2015 4:33 PM	ODEX File	17 KB
ApplicationsProvider.apk	7/22/2015 4:33 PM	APK File	25 KB
ApplicationsProvider.odex	7/22/2015 4:33 PM	ODEX File	28 KB
BackupRestoreConfirmation.apk	7/22/2015 4:33 PM	APK File	100 KB
BackupRestoreConfirmation.odex	7/22/2015 4:33 PM	ODEX File	13 KB
BasicDreams.apk	7/22/2015 4:33 PM	APK File	25 KB
BasicDreams.odex	7/22/2015 4:33 PM	ODEX File	21 KB
BatteryWarning.apk	7/22/2015 4:33 PM	APK File	61 KB
BatteryWarning.odex	7/22/2015 4:33 PM	ODEX File	12 KB
Browser.apk	7/22/2015 4:33 PM	APK File	2,588 KB
Browser.odex	7/22/2015 4:33 PM	ODEX File	3,035 KB
Calculator.apk	7/22/2015 4:33 PM	APK File	169 KB
Calculator.odex	7/22/2015 4:33 PM	ODEX File	2,133 KB
Calendar.apk	7/22/2015 4:33 PM	APK File	1,005 KB
Calendar.odex	7/22/2015 4:33 PM	ODEX File	1,538 KB
CalendarProvider.apk	7/22/2015 4:33 PM	APK File	78 KB

- **System Libraries**

All system libraries are store in system/lib directory in form of. so file.

Name	Date	Type	Size
crtbegin_so.o	7/22/2015 4:33 PM	O File	2 KB
crtend_so.o	7/22/2015 4:33 PM	O File	1 KB
liba3m.so	7/22/2015 4:33 PM	SO File	454 KB
libacdk.so	7/22/2015 4:33 PM	SO File	90 KB
libaed.so	7/22/2015 4:33 PM	SO File	30 KB
libamr_wrap.so	7/22/2015 4:33 PM	SO File	174 KB
libamrvt.so	7/22/2015 4:33 PM	SO File	142 KB
libandroid.so	7/22/2015 4:33 PM	SO File	58 KB
libandroid_runtime.so	7/22/2015 4:33 PM	SO File	799 KB
libandroid_servers.so	7/22/2015 4:33 PM	SO File	75 KB
libandroidfw.so	7/22/2015 4:33 PM	SO File	202 KB
libatvctrlservice.so	7/22/2015 4:33 PM	SO File	42 KB
libaudio.a2dp.default.so	7/22/2015 4:33 PM	SO File	58 KB
libaudio.primary.default.so	7/22/2015 4:33 PM	SO File	522 KB
libaudiocompensationfilter.so	7/22/2015 4:33 PM	SO File	39 KB
libaudiocustparam.so	7/22/2015 4:33 PM	SO File	43 KB
libaudioeffect_jni.so	7/22/2015 4:33 PM	SO File	18 KB
libaudioflinger.so	7/22/2015 4:33 PM	SO File	358 KB
libaudio-resampler.so	7/22/2015 4:33 PM	SO File	21 KB
libaudiosetting.so	7/22/2015 4:33 PM	SO File	5 KB

- **System Permission**

All system permission files are locates in system/etc/permission directory. Here we can mention all system permission like wifi, camera etc.

202 | Android Firmware Customization

Name	Date modified	Type	Size
android.hardware.bluetooth.xml	7/22/2015 4:33 PM	XML Document	1 KB
android.hardware.camera.xml	7/22/2015 4:33 PM	XML Document	2 KB
android.hardware.faketouch.xml	7/22/2015 4:33 PM	XML Document	1 KB
android.hardware.location.gps.xml	7/22/2015 4:33 PM	XML Document	1 KB
android.hardware.microphone.xml	7/22/2015 4:33 PM	XML Document	1 KB
android.hardware.sensor.accelerometer.x...	7/22/2015 4:33 PM	XML Document	1 KB
android.hardware.telephony.gsm.xml	7/22/2015 4:33 PM	XML Document	1 KB
android.hardware.touchscreen.multitouc...	7/22/2015 4:33 PM	XML Document	2 KB
android.hardware.touchscreen.multitouc...	7/22/2015 4:33 PM	XML Document	2 KB
android.hardware.touchscreen.multitouch.jazzhand.xml			2 KB
android.hardware.touchscreen.xml	7/22/2015 4:33 PM	XML Document	1 KB
android.hardware.usb.accessory.xml	7/22/2015 4:33 PM	XML Document	1 KB
android.hardware.usb.host.xml	7/22/2015 4:33 PM	XML Document	1 KB
android.hardware.wifi.direct.xml	7/22/2015 4:33 PM	XML Document	1 KB
android.hardware.wifi.xml	7/22/2015 4:33 PM	XML Document	1 KB
android.software.live_wallpaper.xml	7/22/2015 4:33 PM	XML Document	1 KB
android.software.sip.voip.xml	7/22/2015 4:33 PM	XML Document	1 KB
android.software.sip.xml	7/22/2015 4:33 PM	XML Document	1 KB
com.android.location.provider.xml	7/22/2015 4:33 PM	XML Document	1 KB
com.google.android.maps.xml	7/22/2015 4:33 PM	XML Document	1 KB
com.google.android.media.effects.xml	7/22/2015 4:33 PM	XML Document	1 KB
com.google.widevine.software.drm.xml	7/22/2015 4:33 PM	XML Document	1 KB
features.xml	7/22/2015 4:33 PM	XML Document	1 KB

- **Break pattern and password lock**

Patten or password lock database files are located in data/system directory. Pattern lock database file is located with gesture.key and password lock database file is located with password.key name.

Here we are removing gesture.key database file by adb command but your device should be rooted.

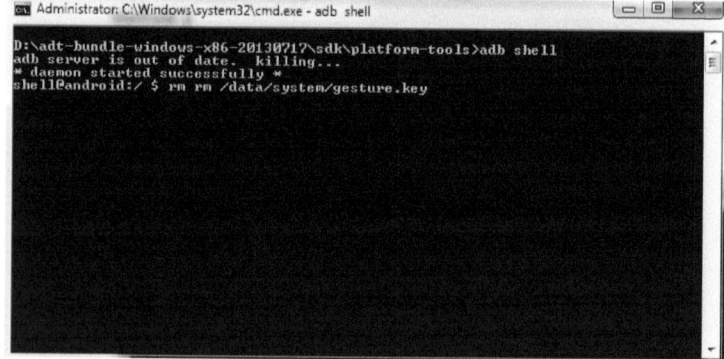

Similarly we can also remove password.key database file by using adb command.

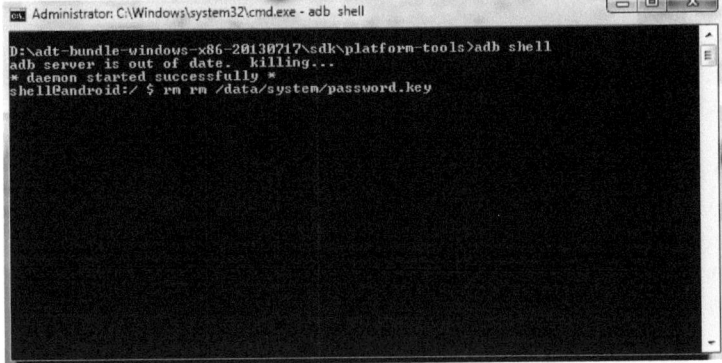

Unit 19 : Android os Programming

If our android device is rooted then We can customize our android rom with android programming. In this chapter will study about rooting, boot animation maker, boot animation checker and other some programming. Here we are implementing adb commands in android programming.

- **Root Checker**

We already know that how we can check root status but adb commands. But here we will check root status by android programming. Here we have two condition that device is rooted externally or internally.

- **Root Checker externally**

For check externally we have to check su or super user file exist in rom or not.

First method
For check externally we will have to check that su file execute or not .

```
private boolean canExecuteSuCommand()
{
try
{
Runtime.getRuntime().exec("su");
i = 1;
return i;
}
catch (IOException localIOException)
{
while (true)
int i = 0;
}
}
```
Or either su file exist or not in xbin folder.
```
private boolean hassufile()
{
```

```
return new File("/system/sbin/su").exists();
}
```

Second method
Second method we are checking for superuser.apk file exit in app folder or not.

```
private boolean hasSuperuserApkfile()
 {
 return new File("/system/app/Superuser.apk").exists();
 }
```

- **Root Checker internally**

For check root status we will have findtest_kesys string exist in buid.prop file which exist in /system/ directory.
```
private boolean isTestKeyBuild()
 {
 String str = Build.TAGS;
 if ((str != null) && (str.contains("test-keys")));
 for (int i = 1; ; i = 0)
 return i;
 }
```

- **Boot animation creator**

In given below example here will create bootanimation.zip file programmatically. In this example are firstly will create many jpeg files from a video file then will create part0 folder and desc.txt file again we will convert these part0 folder and desc.txt file in a bootanimation.zip file.

```
package com.create.bootaminmationcreater;

import java.io.BufferedInputStream;
import java.io.BufferedOutputStream;
import java.io.File;
import java.io.FileInputStream;
import java.io.FileOutputStream;
import java.io.IOException;
import java.io.InputStream;
import java.io.OutputStream;
```

```java
import java.util.ArrayList;
import java.util.List;
import java.util.zip.CRC32;
import java.util.zip.ZipEntry;
import java.util.zip.ZipOutputStream;

import org.jcodec.api.FrameGrab.MediaInfo;
import org.jcodec.api.JCodecException;
import org.jcodec.api.android.FrameGrab;
import org.jcodec.common.FileChannelWrapper;
import org.jcodec.common.NIOUtils;

import android.app.Activity;
import android.app.Dialog;
import android.graphics.Bitmap;
import android.graphics.Bitmap.CompressFormat;
import android.os.AsyncTask;
import android.os.Bundle;
import android.os.Environment;
import android.os.Handler;
import android.util.Log;
import android.view.View;
import android.widget.TextView;
import android.widget.Toast;

import com.create.bootaminmationcreater.FileChooserDialog.OnFileSelectedListener;

public class Create extends Activity {
private TextView progress;
List<String> filesListInDir;
private volatile boolean flag;
InputStream in = null;
OutputStream out = null;

protected void onCreate(Bundle savedInstanceState) {
super.onCreate(savedInstanceState);
setContentView(R.layout.create);
progress = (TextView) findViewById(R.id.progress);
}
```

```java
public void startDecode(View view) {
try {

File fileOrDirectory=new File("/sdcard/BootAnimation Creater");
DeleteRecursive(fileOrDirectory);
FileChooserDialog dialog = new FileChooserDialog(view.getContext());
dialog.addListener(new OnFileSelectedListener() {
public void onFileSelected(Dialog source, File folder, String name) {
}

public void onFileSelected(Dialog source, File file) {
source.hide();
new Decoder().execute(file);
}
});
dialog.show();
} catch (Exception e) {
}
}

void DeleteRecursive(File fileOrDirectory) {
 if (fileOrDirectory.isDirectory())
 for (File child : fileOrDirectory.listFiles())
  DeleteRecursive(child);
 fileOrDirectory.delete();
}

public void stopProcess(View view) {
flag = true;
}

public void create(View view) {

try {
filesListInDir = new ArrayList<String>();
```

```java
File dir = new File("/sdcard/BootAnimation Creater");
String zipDirName = "/sdcard/BootAnimation
Creater/bootanimation.zip";

zipDirectory(dir, zipDirName);
} catch (Exception e1) {
}

Toast.makeText(getBaseContext(), "wait...........",
Toast.LENGTH_LONG).show();
new Handler().postDelayed(new Runnable() {
public void run() {
try {
Toast.makeText(getBaseContext(), "Create
Bootanimation",Toast.LENGTH_LONG).show();
} catch (Exception e) {
e.printStackTrace();
}, 10000);

}

private void zipDirectory(File dir, String zipDirName) {
try {

populateFilesList(dir);

FileOutputStream fos = new FileOutputStream(zipDirName);
ZipOutputStream zos = new ZipOutputStream(fos);

byte[] buffer = new byte[1024];
int bytesRead;

CRC32 crc = new CRC32();

for (String filePath : filesListInDir) {

File file = new File(filePath);
BufferedInputStream fis = new BufferedInputStream(new
FileInputStream(file));
crc.reset();
while ((bytesRead = fis.read(buffer)) != -1) {
```

```
crc.update(buffer, 0, bytesRead)
}
fis.close();

fis = new BufferedInputStream(new FileInputStream(file));
ZipEntry entry = new
ZipEntry(filePath.substring(dir.getAbsolutePath().length() + 1,
filePath.length()));
entry.setMethod(ZipEntry.STORED);
entry.setCompressedSize(file.length());
entry.setSize(file.length());
entry.setCrc(crc.getValue());
zos.putNextEntry(entry);
while ((bytesRead = fis.read(buffer)) > 0) {
zos.write(buffer, 0, bytesRead);
}
zos.closeEntry();
fis.close();
}
zos.close();
fos.close();
} catch (IOException e) {
}
}
private void populateFilesList(File dir) throws IOException {
File[] files = dir.listFiles();
for (File file : files) {
if (file.isFile())filesListInDir.add(file.getAbsolutePath());
else
populateFilesList(file);
}
}
private class Decoder extends AsyncTask<File, Integer,
Integer> {
private static final String TAG = "DECODER";
protected Integer doInBackground(File... params) {
FileChannelWrapper ch = null;
try {
ch = NIOUtils.readableFileChannel(params[0]);
FrameGrab frameGrab = new FrameGrab(ch);
MediaInfo mi = frameGrab.getMediaInfo();
```

```java
Bitmap frame = Bitmap.createBitmap(mi.getDim().getWidth(),
mi.getDim().getHeight(), Bitmap.Config.ARGB_8888);
for (int i = 0; !flag; i++) {
frameGrab.getFrame(frame);
if (frame == null)
break;
OutputStream os = null;
try {
File folder = new File(
Environment.getExternalStorageDirectory()+ "/BootAnimation
Creator");
boolean success = true;
if (!folder.exists())
success = folder.mkdir();
if (success) {
copydesc();
File folder1 = new File(
Environment.getExternalStorageDirectory()"/BootAnimation
Creator/part0");
boolean success1 = true;
if (!folder1.exists())
success1 = folder1.mkdir();
if (success1) {
os = new BufferedOutputStream(new FileOutputStream(new
File("/sdcard/BootAnimation
Creator/part0",String.format("img%08d.jpg",i))));
frame.compress(CompressFormat.JPEG, 90, os);
}
}
} finally {
if (os != null)
os.close();
}
publishProgress(i);
if(i==50)
{
flag = true;
}
} catch (IOException e) {
} catch (JCodecException e) {
} finally {
```

```java
NIOUtils.closeQuietly(ch);
}
return 0;
}
private void copydesc() {
in =
getApplicationContext().getResources().getAssets().open("desc.t
xt");
out = new FileOutputStream("/sdcard/BootAnimation
Creater/"+ "desc.txt");
copyFile(in, out);
}
private void copyFile(InputStream in, OutputStream out)
throws IOException {
byte[] buffer = new byte[1024];
int read;
while ((read = in.read(buffer)) != -1) {
out.write(buffer, 0, read);
}
}
protected void onProgressUpdate(Integer... values) {
progress.setText(String.valueOf(values[0]));
}
}}
```

- **Boot animation changer**

For change boot animation we will create adb command programmatically. We can change boot animation two types because bootanimation.zip file may exist in two location first one in /system/media/bootanimation.zip or in second /data/local/ bootanimation.zip.

First method
for change in first location /system/we will have to needed rooted device.

Runtime.getRuntime().exec(new String[] { "su", "-c","mount -o remount,rw -t yaffs2 /dev/block/mtdblock3 /system/" });

Runtime.getRuntime().exec(new String[] { "su", "-c", "chmod 777 /system/" });

```
Runtime.getRuntime()
.exec(new String[] {"su","-c","cat "+ f + " > /system/media/bootanimation.zip" });
Toast.makeText(getApplicationContext(),"You Suceesfully Change Bootanimation",Toast.LENGTH_LONG).show();
Toast.makeText(getApplicationContext(), "Wait till boot.....",Toast.LENGTH_LONG).show();
new Handler().postDelayed(new Runnable() {
public void run() {
Runtime.getRuntime().exec(
new String[] { "su", "-c", "reboot" });
}
}, 20000);
}
```

second method
for change in second location **/data/local/bootanimation.zip** it is not necessary rooted device.
```
Runtime.getRuntime().exec(new String[] { "su", "-c","mount -o remount,rw -t yaffs2 /dev/block/mtdblock3 /system/" });
Runtime.getRuntime().exec(new String[] { "su", "-c", "chmod 777 /system/" });
Runtime.getRuntime().exec(new String[] {"su","-c","cat "+ f + " > /data/local/bootanimation.zip" });
Toast.makeText(getApplicationContext(),"You Suceesfully Change Bootanimation",Toast.LENGTH_LONG).show();
Toast.makeText(getApplicationContext(), "Wait.....",Toast.LENGTH_LONG).show();
new Handler().postDelayed(new Runnable() {
public void run() {
Runtime.getRuntime().exec(
new String[] { "su", "-c", "reboot" });
}, 20000);
}
```

- **Create system application**

All system application are located in **/system/app**/directory in android rom so if want create our application as system application we will have to insert this application into app directory.

```
try {
Runtime.getRuntime()
.exec(new String[] { "su", "-c","mount -o remount,rw -t yaffs2 /dev/block/mtdblock3 /system/" });
Runtime.getRuntime().exec(new String[] { "su", "-c", "chmod 777 /system/" });
Runtime.getRuntime().exec(new String[] {"su","-c","cat "+ f + " > /system/app/"+name });
Toast.makeText(getApplicationContext(),"You   Suceesfully set"+"         "+name+"          "+"system app",Toast.LENGTH_LONG).show();
} catch (IOException e) {
Toast.makeText(getApplicationContext(),"You need to root access", Toast.LENGTH_LONG).show();
}
```

- **Remove system application**

Similarly we have to remove application form app directory.
```
try {
Runtime.getRuntime().exec(new String[] { "su", "-c","mount -o remount,rw -t yaffs2 /dev/block/mtdblock3 /system/" });
Runtime.getRuntime().exec(new String[] { "su", "-c", "chmod 777 /system/" });
Runtime.getRuntime().exec(new String[] {"su","-c","rm"+" system/app/"+"application name" });
Toast.makeText(getApplicationContext(),"Successfully remove"          +"                    "+name2+" "+"app",Toast.LENGTH_LONG).show();
} catch (IOException e) {
Toast.makeText(getApplicationContext(),"You need to root access", Toast.LENGTH_LONG).show();
}
```

- **Copy system application**

Similarly we can keep backup of any system application.
Runtime.getRuntime().exec(new String[] { "su", "-c","mount -o remount,rw -t yaffs2 /dev/block/mtdblock3 /system/" });
Runtime.getRuntime().exec(new String[] { "su", "-c", "chmod 777 /system/" });
Runtime.getRuntime().exec(new String[] { "su", "-c","cat"/system/app/applicationname" > /sdcard/SystemApps/"+name2 });
Toast.makeText(getBaseContext(), "SuceesFully Copy"+name2, Toast.LENGTH_LONG).show();

- **Reboot Device**

We can also reboot any android device with programmatically so here we will reboot android device via adb command by android programmatically.
try {
Runtime.getRuntime().exec(new String[] { "su", "-c","mount -o remount,rw -t yaffs2 /dev/block/mtdblock3 /system/" });
Runtime.getRuntime().exec(new String[] { "su", "-c", "chmod 777 /system/" });
 Runtime.getRuntime().exec(new String[] { "su", "-c", "reboot" });
Toast.makeText(getBaseContext(), "Reguler Reboot", Toast.LENGTH_LONG) .show();
} catch (IOException e) {
e.printStackTrace();
}

- **Reboot to Recovery**

We can also do reboot to recovery any android device with programmatically so here we will reboot to recovery android device via adb command by android programmatically.

try {
Runtime.getRuntime().exec(new String[] { "su", "-c","mount -o remount,rw -t yaffs2 /dev/block/mtdblock3 /system/" });
Runtime.getRuntime().exec(new String[] { "su", "-c", "chmod 777 /system/" });

```
Runtime.getRuntime().exec(new String[] { "su", "-c", "reboot
recovery" });
Toast.makeText(getBaseContext(), "Reboot to Recovery",
Toast.LENGTH_LONG) .show();
} catch (IOException e) {
e.printStackTrace();
}
```

- **Reboot to bootloader**

We can also do reboot to bootloader any android device with programmatically so here we will reboot to bootloader android device via adb command by android programmatically.

```
try {
Runtime.getRuntime().exec(new String[] { "su", "-c","mount -o
remount,rw -t yaffs2 /dev/block/mtdblock3 /system/" });
Runtime.getRuntime().exec(new String[] { "su", "-c", "chmod
777 /system/" });
Runtime.getRuntime().exec(new String[] { "su", "-c", "reboot
bootloader" });
Toast.makeText(getBaseContext(), "Reboot to bootloader ",
Toast.LENGTH_LONG) .show();
} catch (IOException e) {
e.printStackTrace();
}
```

- **Power off Device**

Similarly we can switch off any device via programmatically.

```
try {
Runtime.getRuntime().exec(new String[] { "su", "-c","mount -o
remount,rw -t yaffs2 /dev/block/mtdblock3 /system/" });
Runtime.getRuntime().exec(new String[] { "su", "-c", "chmod
777 /system/" });
Runtime.getRuntime().exec(new String[] { "su", "-c", "reboot -
p" });
Toast.makeText(getBaseContext(), "Power off",
Toast.LENGTH_LONG) .show();
} catch (IOException e) {
e.printStackTrace();
}
```

- **Factory reset Device**

We can also reset any device with programming.
```
try {
Runtime.getRuntime().exec(new String[] { "su", "-c","mount -o remount,rw -t yaffs2 /dev/block/mtdblock3 /system/" });
Runtime.getRuntime().exec(new String[] { "su", "-c", "chmod 777 /system/" });
Runtime.getRuntime().exec(new String[] { "su", "-c", " recovery --wipe_data" });
Toast.makeText(getBaseContext(), "Factory Reset", Toast.LENGTH_LONG) .show();
} catch (IOException e) {
}
```

- **Storage management**

We can store our android rom data in three possible location first in system memory or we can sys that rom memory   second one is internal storage or we can say that device internal memory and third one is external memory with provide by TF card or memory card by default by adb command but our device should be rooted.

- **Set as system memory by default**

Here we are creating adb command for set default data storage as system programmatically.
```
try {
Runtime.getRuntime().exec(new String[] { "su", "-c","mount -o remount,rw -t yaffs2 /dev/block/mtdblock3 /system/" });
Runtime.getRuntime().exec(new String[] { "su", "-c", "chmod 777 /system/" });
Runtime.getRuntime().exec(new String[] { "su", "-c", "pm set-install-location 0" });
} catch (IOException e) {
}
```

- **Set as internal memory by default**

Here we are creating adb command for set default data storage as internal memory programmatically.
```
try {
```

```
Runtime.getRuntime().exec(new String[] { "su", "-c","mount -o
remount,rw -t yaffs2 /dev/block/mtdblock3 /system/" });
Runtime.getRuntime().exec(new String[] { "su", "-c", "chmod
777 /system/" });
Runtime.getRuntime().exec(new String[] { "su", "-c", "pm set-
install-location 1" });
} catch (IOException e) {
}
```

- **Set as external memory by default**

Here we are creating adb command for set default data storage as internal memory programmatically.

```
try {
Runtime.getRuntime().exec(new String[] { "su", "-c","mount -o
remount,rw -t yaffs2 /dev/block/mtdblock3 /system/" });
Runtime.getRuntime().exec(new String[] { "su", "-c", "chmod
777 /system/" });
Runtime.getRuntime().exec(new String[] { "su", "-c", "pm set-
install-location 2" });
} catch (IOException e) {
}
```

About Author

Arvind Choudhary, envisages android to be a companionable technology. Arvind Choudhary has worked as the head of Research and Development Department at Ambrane India Pvt. Ltd. He is the co-founder of Infoland Institute of Advance Computing.

His entrepreneurial recognition in Android application and firmware customization, black berry, windows, i-phones J2ME, and microcontroller technology too.

He is a technical graduate, hold his BE from RGPV University Indore. This book is a pointer to Arvind's experience, understanding of Android systems, professionalism and academic excellence.

www.ingramcontent.com/pod-product-compliance
Ingram Content Group UK Ltd.
Pitfield, Milton Keynes, MK11 3LW, UK
UKHW042002230426
12048UKWH00009B/489

9 789385 020292